MW00627046

"My friend Doug Garasic's new book *Wayside* is a must-read for anyone who feels stuck in a mess. As Doug walks us through the life of Bartimaeus I can't help but see myself and many others who can identify with this story. I'll say it again: THIS IS A MUST-READ!"

PERRY NOBLE
NEW YORK TIMES BEST-SELLING AUTHOR
PASTOR OF SECOND CHANCE CHURCH

"What I love most about my friend, Doug Garasic, is his passion to see people fully alive and thriving in all that they do. Those are the type of people I want to surround myself with and speak into my life. All of us have felt stuck at some point and have faced roads that seem daunting. It's part the journey of following God. What you do in those moments matter. You will never reach your destiny if you remain stuck and crippled by labels, circumstances, or anything else that comes your way. *Wayside* is a book written from a place of raw honesty, vulnerability, and hope that will infuse courage into the hearts of those who know there is more and want to step into all that God has for them."

BANNING LIEBSCHER
FOUNDER & PASTOR OF JESUS CULTURE

"'God does some of his best work in our worst moments.' When I read this from Doug in *Wayside*, I couldn't agree more."

DINO RIZZO
AUTHOR OF *SERVOLUTION* & EXECUTIVE DIRECTOR OF
ASSOCIATION OF RELATED CHURCHES (ARC)

"The world, the culture, and life's circumstances will all do their best to defeat you, deny you, or at least, distort you according to what 'they' say is best. But Doug Garasic understands that through it all, even in what seem like the worst moments of your life, God is at work. And his work in you is always masterful and original. In his book, *Wayside*, Doug will encourage you, challenge you, and cheer you to victory as you continue your own journey of discovery and destiny."

ROD PARSLEY
NEW YORK TIMES BEST-SELLING AUTHOR
PASTOR OF WORLD HARVEST CHURCH

DOUGLAS J. GARASIC

WAY
SIDE

THE LAST PLACE YOU'D
EXPECT TO FIND GOD

 KOPI
BOOKS

WAYSIDE
Published by Kopi Books
105B 5555 Youngstown Warren Road
Niles, OH 44446 U.S.A.

Unless otherwise indicated, all Scripture quotations are taken from Holy Bible, New Living Translation, copyright © 1996, 2004, 2015 by Tyndale House Foundation. Used by permission of Tyndale House Publishers, Inc., Carol Stream, Illinois 60188. All rights reserved.

Scripture quotation of Mark 10:46 at the beginning of chapter 2, and the phrase "by the wayside," is sourced from the Darby Bible. Public domain.

Scripture quotations marked NIV are from the Holy Bible, New International Version®, NIV® Copyright © 1973, 1978, 1984, 2011 by Biblica, Inc.® Used by permission. All rights reserved worldwide.

Scripture quotations marked MSG are taken from The Message, copyright © 1993, 2002, 2018 by Eugene H. Peterson. Used by permission of NavPress. All rights reserved. Represented by Tyndale House Publishers, Inc.

Scripture quotations marked KJV are from The King James Version. Public Domain.

Scripture quotations marked TPT are from The Passion Translation®. Copyright © 2017 by Passion & Fire Ministries, Inc. Used by permission. All rights reserved. thePassionTranslation.com

ISBN 978-0-578-22471-8

The Team: Stephanie Garasic, Brad Tarleton
Cover Design: Lydia Tarleton

Printed in the United States of America
2019

FOR EVERY PERSON
WHO FEELS LIKE YOUR MESS
IS TOO BIG FOR GOD'S MERCY—
I WROTE THIS BOOK FOR YOU

CONTENTS

FOREWORD

Undoubtedly, one of my favorite moments was meeting this young fiery red-headed preacher. He seemed to break every mold and stereotype in a world where we often portray that we "have it all together" or have attained ultimate success or notoriety, Doug busted into my world as a refreshing surprise.

We all want good things to happen in our lives, but too often we want it now, not later. We also feel we know how it should finally play out in our lives but instead what happens in the wait is enough to drive us crazy.

Doug will invite you into the messy parts of his story, not to revel in his crazy narrative (because that is in here, too) but in his absolute passion and determination to help others on the journey to get unstuck, deal with anger, let go of labels, frustration, rejection, and doubt about your purpose and God's dream for you.

God gives us hopes and dreams for certain things to happen in our lives, but he doesn't always allow us to see the exact timing of his plan. After a seed is planted, the heat, moisture and pressure of the soil will finally cause the outer shell to crack open. This book is about that place we all find ourselves in before the truth of God's identity in us breaks through.

For everyone there will come a time, where you will need to choose to hear and act on God's words above the naysayers or the doubters. Trust me this book will be worth reading every word!

I salute my young friend for the work he is doing, and I know his obedience and vulnerability will empower a generation of individuals, leaders, and pastors.

He has, for sure, empowered me.

— PIERRE DUPLESSIS
PASTOR OF THE FATHER'S HOUSE NEW YORK

PROLOGUE

Let me tell you about the worst day of my life.

I was twenty years old and excited about the new season I was entering. I had been in bible college for the last two years – two *long* years. For the first time in my life, I was going to complete something meaningful. I was about to prove that I was more than the negative things people had said about me. I was proud of myself, but most importantly, excited for the future. I had put in the time to learn everything I needed to know about ministry (so I thought) and was ready not only to get out into the world but to change the world!

If everything had gone according to plan, this would be a nice story with a happy ending. However, I don't know about your life, but in my life, nothing ever goes according to plan.

Because of certain things that happened – some I

was at fault for and some I was not – I got kicked out of bible college right before graduation day. I didn't get a degree, certificate, job offer, handshake, or even an "atta boy!" I got nothing. It felt like all of the blood, sweat, and tears that I had put into the last two years of my life were for nothing!

I didn't know how to deal with the slew of emotions that followed. I felt frustrated, disappointed, angry, depressed, abandoned, and terribly hurt. I wanted to lash out at the people who had kicked me to the curb, but I knew that God was calling me to be a bigger person. In moments of clarity between my anger, I could hear the Lord say, "Trust me and walk away."

Since my dreams of doing ministry were shattered, I started working at a fitness center. One of my coworkers, Paul, was not a Christian, so even though I was in a tough season, I was still trying to be an example of Jesus to him. When Paul found out I'd gotten kicked out of bible college, he invited me to hang out that night to try to cheer me up.

Now remember, Paul wasn't a "church friend." Maybe some of you reading this book understand – when "church friends" hang out it's a lot different than when your "other friends" hang out. Let me say it like this: Paul's idea of cheering me up was a lot different than how Jesus would have cheered me up, if you know what I mean.

When I pulled up to Paul's house, I could see that this wasn't so much a "hang out" as it was a full-blown party. There were plenty of girls and even more alcohol

– just the type of banger parties that I used to go to before I met Jesus.

As I was observing the party from my car, an internal tug-of-war began. Should I go in or stay away? Thoughts raced through my mind. *What does it matter? Ministry isn't working out for you. Heck, Jesus isn't really working out for you. Where is he now? Since your plans to serve God fell apart, maybe you should go back to what you used to do.*

I was at the lowest point that I had ever been in my Christianity. The people I had trusted had rejected me, my biggest accomplishment had been taken from me, and honestly it felt like God had forgotten about me. I was stuck. I would never get out of this mess.

Almost at my breaking point, I punched the steering wheel and my knuckles started to bleed. I wanted to give up, get drunk, and be stupid. I wanted to become the person that those who kicked me out of bible college thought I was. I was full of frustration and temptation.

Now, I don't mean to preach in the Prologue (I'm trying to save the good stuff for later) but often in your moments of greatest frustration you'll experience the greatest temptation. The devil always tries to take advantage of you at your weakest.

But in a last-ditch moment of desperation, I started to pray. "God, why am I in this situation? Why do you have me stuck here?"

I felt God whisper to me, "Doug, when you're at your worst, I'm still at my best."

At that moment, with bloody knuckles and tears running down my face, I found the strength from the

Holy Spirit to call Paul, say I couldn't come to the party, and leave.

As I drove away, I felt peace inside of me that only could have come from God. Even though I was in a hopeless situation, he was downloading hope on the inside of me.

IN MY WORST MOMENT, GOD WAS DOING HIS BEST WORK.

Right now, you might be in the middle of one of your worst moments. Your faith might be weak, your relationships struggling, finances lacking, or your life falling apart. It might feel like you've been in a fight with the devil and he's been whooping your butt. And if you're not careful, you'll start to believe the lie that you're stuck where you are. You'll believe that the circumstances are too bad to change, that if God was going to do anything, he would have already shown up by now. You might even believe that because you've been stuck for a while, that's where God wants you. Maybe you think you did something to earn it or deserve it, so you'd better learn to put on a brave face and get comfortable in your mess, because you aren't going anywhere.

The encouragement I have for you is that God can absolutely, one thousand percent do his best work in the middle of your worst moment. Let me share some good news with you, not just from my story, but from the mouth of Jesus: *"I came that they may have life and have it abundantly."* [1]

Jesus came specifically so that you could have abundant life. Abundant life doesn't look like the mess that you're currently in. Jesus didn't go to the cross and defeat the power of sin and the devil for you to remain stuck in the effects of them. He came so that he could pull you out of where you are and lead you into the abundant life that he has reserved for you.

For the remainder of this book, we are going to dive into one of the most powerful stories in the Bible. It's a story that has transformed the way that I live. It's the story of a man named Bartimaeus.

If you feel stuck, I guarantee you that Bartimaeus was stuck worse. However, in spite of his circumstances, he experienced the abundant life that Jesus had for him because he chose to step out in faith and follow Jesus.

This book isn't just a nice message, a cool way to look at a Bible story, or a way to pass your time. The fact that you currently have it in your hands means that God is inviting you to something. He's inviting you to redefine the way that you follow him – to step away from stuck and step into your miracle.

Maybe you didn't know that things could change for you. Maybe you gave up on life getting better. Maybe you have packed away the dreams that God placed on your heart. Maybe you aren't expecting to find God in a fresh, new way.

However, what Bartimaeus learned, what I've learned, and what you're about to learn is this: God often shows up in the last place you'd expect to find him.

GOD OFTEN SHOWS UP IN THE LAST PLACE YOU'D EXPECT TO FIND HIM.

GET READY »

CHAPTER ONE

LABELS

THEN THEY REACHED JERICHO, AND AS JESUS AND HIS DISCIPLES LEFT TOWN, A LARGE CROWD FOLLOWED HIM. A BLIND BEGGAR NAMED BARTIMAEUS...

MARK 10:46

Have you ever been to a ritzy, expensive place before? Maybe a country club or an all-inclusive resort or a fancy restaurant – you can almost *feel* the money there.

As Jesus and his disciples are traveling, they pass through a place like that. At this time, the city of Jericho was home to the rich and powerful. Because of its warm weather and freshwater springs, this "City of Palm Trees" was where King Herod built his winter palace. I envision a place that had amazing restaurants, tons of "touristy" things to do, and ridiculously inflated prices. It was a city available for enjoyment, if you had some cash flow, of course.

I'm not saying there's anything wrong with having money or going to these types of places, but when there's someone there who isn't in the same tax bracket as everyone else, it's pretty noticeable.

Enter Bartimaeus. He was surrounded by paradise, luxury, and people who had money; yet the reality of his situation was drastically different from those around him. He stuck out like a sore thumb. It was a constant reminder of everything that he wasn't. He knew it and everybody else knew it. So much so that he wasn't even called by his name, but by what people had labeled him.

It's interesting that when the Bible describes Bartimaeus his label precedes his name. He isn't referred to as, "Bartimaeus, a blind beggar," but rather "a blind beggar named Bartimaeus." In other words, his label was more important than his name. *What* he was, not *who* he was, took center stage in his life.

I wonder how many of us have been given labels that overshadow who we really are. Before we are known by the birth name that our parents gave us, we are known by the labels that others have placed on us. I don't know your name, but I might be able to guess some labels that have been put on you:

Fat. Dramatic. Broke. Divorced. Lazy. Stupid. Emotional. Mistake. Failure. It doesn't matter who we are or how "perfect" we have tried to be, we all carry at least one label. More than likely, you carry several.

Bartimaeus was labeled "blind" and "beggar," two characteristics that kept him shackled to a life of poverty and neglect, unable to improve his position in life because of what people saw when they looked at him.

You'll find out later in this story that Bartimaeus didn't allow what others had labeled him to define him.

In the same way, your labels don't have to define you.

The thing about a label is that it's always located on the outside of a product. Let's use cereal as an example. When you go to the grocery store and are trying to decide which cereal to buy, you typically choose according to which label looks the most impressive. However, I'll bet there's been a time or two when you opened up the box of cereal, poured the milk, lifted the spoon to your mouth, and the contents didn't match the promise of the label.

In the same way, people tend to judge other people according to what they see on the outside. They judge according to looks, deficiencies, talents, or inabilities. They judge by the past we've had and the mistakes we've made. From a rational perspective, judging by this standard makes sense to us. We all have good and bad qualities, features and flaws, things at which we excel or fall short. How else would people describe us? What they see on the outside becomes the label we carry. That's how the world works. But here's how God works…

When Samuel, who was a prophet, was given the task of anointing the next King of Israel, he thought that God would be impressed by the same things that he was. However, God rejected all of the most impressive candidates, saying, "The Lord doesn't see things the way you see them. People judge by outward appearance, but the Lord looks at the heart."[1]

GOD DOESN'T LABEL US ACCORDING TO THE OUTSIDE, HE LOOKS AT WHAT IS GOING ON INSIDE.

While the world only knows what they see, God knows what he placed on the inside of us and what he wants to pull out of us. Even if we aren't as good-looking, talented or charismatic as the person next to us, if we focus on getting our hearts lined up with God's heart, he can still use us in amazing ways. Don't be surprised when what God does through you, in spite of your label, becomes the thing that shows off his goodness.

SENIOR PASTOR MATERIAL

I was 26 when my wife, Stephanie, and I planted Rust City Church. For the previous five years, we were youth pastors and had considerable success. We built a thriving youth ministry out of nothing, and then moved on to work for a very large church. We made really good money (if you know youth ministry, you know that's rare) and from the world's perspective, we had made it. We could have comfortably chosen to do what we were doing for the rest of our lives.

Even though we were doing well, we believed that God had put a dream in our hearts to plant a church back home in Youngstown, Ohio. So we gave up our beautiful condo, salaries, and social status to move into my parent's basement with our 100-pound dog. As we began the crazy journey of figuring out how in the heck you plant a church, we were excited but also uneasy. This was completely new territory for us, and we knew if God didn't show up in a big way, it wouldn't work!

When we began telling friends and family about our

plans, some of our family members doubted that we had made the right decision. They told Steph that they didn't think I was senior pastor material.

For those of you who might not know what "senior pastor material" is, let me try my best to define it for you. Typically, senior pastors feel somewhat presidential. They know the correct things to say, look well put together, and people naturally want to follow them. They love shaking hands and kissing babies, like someone who would run for office.

I am the opposite of presidential. If you look me up on social media, you will see that I look more like a homeless ginger-hipster.

On top of not looking the part, if I'm being completely transparent, my personality didn't always match the part. I didn't enjoy doing a lot of the stereotypical responsibilities of a senior pastor. Let me rephrase that – I still don't enjoy doing a lot of the stereotypical responsibilities of a senior pastor! For example, people ask pastors for a lot of counseling. Some pastors love walking people through difficult times in life; they do an amazing job showing the compassion of Jesus when people need it the most. Don't get me wrong, I want people to experience this, but when somebody asks me for counseling, my stomach turns. Then there are the weddings, funerals, hospital visits, people asking you to bless their houses…I love people, but I have no natural desire to do those things. That's why I now have campus pastors and staff who excel at these things! However, at that time it was just me and Steph so even though I wasn't wired for it, those responsibilities and expectations would fall on me.

So, let's recap: I didn't look like a senior pastor, I didn't have the personality of a senior pastor, people were saying I shouldn't be a senior pastor behind my back. If you read the prologue, you know I was kicked out of bible college, so I certainly didn't have any qualifications to be a senior pastor. However, even though everything and everyone was saying *no*, I knew that God said *go*.

On the outside I didn't look the part, but I knew that God was stirring up something big on the inside of me. My personality was different than most, but I also knew that my heart for Youngstown was bigger than most. Still, to hear that I wasn't senior pastor material from family was hurtful. The people who were supposed to care about me the most were supporting me the least.

What I've learned is that when God speaks, whatever anybody else said doesn't matter. I had been labeled by the people around me, even the people closest to me. The labels put on me felt like a crushing blow to my identity. However, God, out of his love for me, was still leading me to the very thing that others were sure I couldn't do.

WE CAN BELIEVE WHAT OTHERS HAVE LABELED US OR WHAT GOD'S LOVE SAYS ABOUT US.

I knew that God had put Rust City Church on my heart. It was stronger than any desire I'd ever had before. The Bible says to "take delight in the Lord, and he will give you the desires of your heart."[2] In other words, when our hearts are healthy and fully surrendered to God, he will fill our hearts with desires that please him.

We naturally desire selfish things – that's our sinful nature at work. Therefore, a good gauge to know that you are hearing from God is if you are passionate about something selfless. If it's selfish, it's probably you. If it's selfless, it's probably God.

Leaving the comfort and security of a well-paying job with the hope of helping people find God was the most selfless thing that I had ever done. I knew it was God. So even though it didn't make sense, we moved home into my parents' basement and planted a church.

Today, I'm so glad that I didn't allow the label "not senior pastor material" to stop me.

LABELS ALWAYS TRY TO PROHIBIT YOU FROM THE VERY PLACE GOD HAS PURPOSED FOR YOU.

If I had believed the lie that I was not senior pastor material and never started Rust City Church, who knows if the thousands of salvations and baptisms we've seen over the last eight years would have happened? Who knows if the graduates from Rust City College, our two-year ministry school, would be in ministry making an impact for Jesus now? Who knows if our valley would be seeing some of the hope that it is currently experiencing?

I'm not saying that all of that is because of me. I've already shared with you some of my deficiencies and areas

GOD'S LOVE IS BIGGER THAN MY LABEL

where I come up short. All I'm saying is that God's love is bigger than your label, and unless you give him a chance to overcome the lies you've believed about yourself, you might never know what could have been.

WHO GOD SAYS YOU ARE

Overcoming labels isn't as simple as not believing them or simply pushing past them. You can count on other people, the devil, and even your own mind to remind you of them! If you are going to overcome labels, you have to choose to believe what God says about you. You have to unlearn what you thought to be true by re-learning what is actually true.

It's hard to know what is actually true in life. We live in a culture where the media is often trying to manipulate us to see their side of the story. We scroll through social media feeds and see only the highlight reels of people's lives, only what they want you to see. Deciphering real truth can be difficult!

God has given us an amazing resource to figure out what is true. The Bible, or the Word of God, is exactly what its name says it is – God's words that he gave us so we can get to know him. 2 Timothy 3:16 says,

> *All Scripture is inspired by God and is useful to teach us what is true and to make us realize what is wrong in our lives.*

The Bible was written by men, but those men were under

the inspiration of the Holy Spirit. It was created to be the "true north" for our lives.

Think about this: when God was inspiring the authors of the Bible, he had you in mind! God is omniscient, all-knowing, so he knew who you were and what you would go through before you even physically existed. He knew what guidelines, encouragement, and comfort you'd need to face every obstacle you would encounter.

God knew every label that would be put on you. He knew every negative thing that people would say about you. He knew the lies that the devil would whisper to you. He knew what you would believe about yourself.

Within its 31,103 verse, the Bible contains 30,000 promises from God for his children.[3] It's crazy to think that there are almost as many promises as there are verses! You can't tell me that God doesn't love you when he has so much to say about who he created you to be.

In all of his infinite wisdom, God chose to fill the Bible with a bunch of promises that are intended to show who you are as his follower. If you grab ahold of these promises, they will help you toss aside the labels you've been living under and walk in the freedom of your true identity. Here are just a few:

> For we are God's masterpiece. He has created us anew in Christ Jesus, so we can do the good things he planned for us long ago. (Ephesians 2:10)

> This means that anyone who belongs to Christ has

become a new person. The old life is gone; a new life has begun! (2 Corinthians 5:17)

I no longer call you slaves, because a master doesn't confide in his slaves. Now you are my friends, since I have told you everything the Father told me. (John 15:15)

But to all who believed him and accepted him, he gave the right to become children of God. (John 1:12)

So now you are no longer strangers and foreigners. You are citizens along with all of God's holy people. You are members of God's family. (Ephesians 2:19)

And now there is nothing between you and Father God, for he sees you as holy, flawless, and restored. (Colossians 1:22 TPT)

How precious are your thoughts about me, O God. They cannot be numbered. I can't even count them; they outnumber the grains of sand! (Psalm 139:17-18)

Often we believe the very opposite of what God actually says about us. You may feel insignificant but God says you're a masterpiece. You may feel ashamed of things that you've done but God says you're a new creation. You may feel lonely but God says you are his friend. You may feel abandoned but God says you are his child. You may feel outcast but God says you are a part of his family. You may feel like a failure but God says you're flawless. You may feel unlovable but God says you are precious and he can't stop thinking about you!

WE CAN CHOOSE TO BELIEVE THE LABELS OF THE WORLD OR WE CAN CHOOSE TO BELIEVE THE LABELS OF THE WORD.

Are you willing to reject the lies you've been told and accept what God says about you?

MEN AND WOMEN OF GOD

When I was in bible college, one of the leaders who really impacted my life was Pastor Kevin. He had a rough upbringing but an incredible story. He was a graduate of Teen Challenge, a Christian-based recovery program, whom God had delivered from some pretty heavy stuff. He understood what it was like to be labeled an addict and allow God to redefine who he was.

There is one particular thing I remember about Pastor Kevin. Every time he would see one of the bible college students, he would greet us with his loud, deep voice: "Doug Garasic, man of God! How are you, man of God? What's going on in your life today, man of God?"

There was never a time when he didn't call us men or women of God. To him, that was our identity.

Did I actually feel like a man of God every time

he called me "man of God?" Absolutely not. There were moments when I was struggling and had a hard time accepting that title because it didn't seem as if I was living up to it. In those times, Pastor Kevin would always say to us: "You choose what you believe about yourself. I know by what the Bible says that you are a man of God because you said yes to him and the plans that he has for your life."

I wonder how many of us need some Pastor Kevin encouragement in our lives. Well, let me give it to you: you get to choose what to believe about yourself!

For some reading this, maybe the best prayer that you can pray is: *God, help me see myself as the man or woman of God that you've created me to be.* For others, maybe you have already started to recognize and live in your God-given identity, and now God is inviting you to be a Pastor Kevin for somebody else. There are people all around you who are wrestling with the labels that have been placed on them. They need to know the Truth. They need to know how God feels about them, and how he created them. As you discover who you are in Christ, God wants you to help others find that same freedom. Their change in identity could start by you seeing and speaking about them differently.

Maybe you need to overcome a label. Maybe you need to help someone else overcome their label. Regardless of which position you are in, labels are lies we all have to face.

Bartimaeus was only thought of as "blind beggar" and never more than that, but we'll see later that when he encountered Jesus, the lies that bound him fell away.

Imagine the freedom we'd find if our labels were removed. Imagine how powerful it would be if we lived with confidence in who God says we are. Let's choose God's Word over the words others have spoken about us. Let's choose his love over labels.

ONE
REFLECTION+APPLICATION

What labels have been placed on you? What have you accepted as a part of your identity that doesn't line up with what God says?

_____

_____

_____

What have your labels prevented you from doing? What dreams would you pursue if you didn't feel prohibited by your labels?

_____

_____

_____

What's one Scripture that you can cling to as a reminder of what God thinks about you?

_____

_____

_____

Do you judge other people by their labels? Ask God to help you see and treat them the way that he does.

_____

_____

_____

CHAPTER TWO

BY THE WAYSIDE

...
WAS
SITTING
BY
THE
WAYSIDE.

MARK 10:46

As Jesus and his disciples were leaving Jericho, they walked past the blind beggar Bartimaeus. The Bible says that he "was sitting by the wayside."[1]

You might be wondering why there's a whole chapter based on five words in a seemingly insignificant portion of the Scripture. At first glance, this part of the verse seems unimportant. It gives us a visual that Bartimaeus is sitting down when Jesus passes, but that's about it. Some translations simply say he's sitting by the side of the road. But when I read this particular passage, the phrase "by the wayside" really stuck out to me. The Holy Spirit was tugging on my heart and at first I couldn't understand why.

As I began researching what the "wayside" meant, I knew that what I was learning had the power to change my life. So much so that *Wayside* is what I titled this book. Make sure that you tune in during this chapter because I know that this has the power to change your life, too!

THE WAYSIDE

In the time that Jesus walked the earth, the Roman Empire was the dominant power in much of the world. They ruled over everything surrounding the Mediterranean Sea – what is now Europe, Northern Africa, and also the Middle East, where the stories about Jesus in the Bible take place.

Romans were very advanced in their engineering, especially in their road and water systems. Most larger cities, like Jericho, had a main road that the upper-class citizens would use. On the road, there were merchants lined up where people could buy food, produce, linens, and art. It would be similar to walking past vendors on the streets of New York City.

The Roman Empire was also the first to build waterway systems through many of their cities. Lined up alongside the main road there were freshwater ditches to carry water to the rich houses in Jericho. Beyond the freshwater ditches, there was another set of ditches called the wayside, more accurately defined as the "waste side."

It was the sewage system that ran through Jericho. You can imagine what was in the ditches of the wayside.

Here's where this history lesson has significant meaning in understanding the story of Bartimaeus. He was not sitting by the main road where the merchants were selling and the wealthy bought their goods. He was not even sitting near the freshwater ditch. Bartimaeus was sitting by the wayside. He was right next to the sewer. The place where all of Jericho's crap (am I allowed to say that?) was carried out of the city is the place he resided. He lived his life sitting by waste.

Despite my childhood dream of becoming a Teenage Mutant Ninja Turtle, I really haven't spent too much time hanging out in sewers, but I can imagine that it would be a pretty depressing way to spend your day. What made it even worse was that Bartimaeus' location was a representation of his situation in life.

Bartimaeus was blind and therefore dependent on the pity and charity of others to survive. Because of his impairment, he couldn't get a job and couldn't contribute to society. He'd never experienced things that most of us take for granted. He'd never seen the beauty of nature, art, or the people around him. In a time when technology was not yet developed, a blind man was severely limited in what he could do, so he was forced to beg for money and food.

On top of that, if you remember the last chapter, Bartimaeus was labeled. He was known only as a blind beggar. People judged him solely based on his condition without ever getting to know him. He wasn't spoken to or interacted with as a normal human being; rather, every relationship was affected by the bad hand that life had dealt him.

So Bartimaeus was sitting by crap. Why? Because

when you feel hopeless you tend to surround yourself with more hopelessness. When you are depressed, dark environments are the ones you seek. Bartimaeus is sitting by crap because he feels like crap.

Have you ever felt like that before? Maybe right now you're in the middle of a crappy situation. Maybe you're in the middle of a mess that you don't know how to clean up. Maybe you've been there so long that you've stopped even trying to get out of it.

It might be distance in your marriage, failure at work or school, an upside-down financial situation, or a sin that has entangled you for a very long time. I don't know what your "crap" is. What I do know is that, even though Bartimaeus was sitting by the wayside, Jesus showed up. In the same way, Jesus isn't afraid to show up by the wayside where you've been sitting.

MEANING IN THE MESS

I don't particularly enjoy dealing with crap. I'm not talking about hypothetical crap now, I'm talking about actual crap! The kind of crap that comes out of the human body.

When my youngest son, Ian, was wearing diapers, he had this incredible ability to continuously project his poop outside of them. For my fellow parents out there, you know this is referred to as a "blowout."

It was unbelievable to me! Regardless of how well we put on the diaper or how securely we fastened it, more often than not, we would find poop leaking out. Let me be a little bit more graphic to accurately paint the picture, in case I haven't been graphic enough already. We would find poop running all the way up his back! I would often think that the Olympics should have created a sport for babies to see who could blow out their diapers the best. I have no doubt that Ian could have won the gold.

What you have to know about me is that I'm a germaphobe. I am horribly grossed out by having to see, let alone clean up, anything that comes out of another person, even my own children. I don't care if it's snot, vomit, poop – I can't cope. Because of this, my saintly wife would most frequently deal with these situations, efficiently using three to four wipes at most to clean up an Ian blowout, while I'd use thirty to forty wipes any time I had to change his diaper. If it was my turn to change our son, I'd begin praying harder than I ever had for God's power to intercede in my life. I didn't know if I had the strength to address it!

You can imagine, the blowout situation created intense moments of frustration for me. As it inevitably happened time and time again, I would think, "Dude, I did not sign up for this!"

God will often speak to us in the middle of a mess. In our most frustrated moments, God will pop up and show us that sometimes the problem isn't with our circumstance, the problem is with us.

In the middle of cleaning up a blowout diaper one day, God spoke to me. He said, "Doug, I know you don't like this, but if you didn't have the blowouts, you wouldn't have Ian."

In other words, I could have a life without the mess, but it would also be a life without the blessing of my son.

I began to think about the joy that Ian brought to our family, with his smile that lights up a room and dynamic personality. Being entrusted with raising him has been one of our greatest accomplishments. In that moment, my perspective started to shift.

It was such a powerful revelation for me, especially because my biological father did not raise me. He preferred to avoid the mess of taking care of a child so that he could focus on himself; he chose to be consumed with what he wanted rather than take on the responsibility of parenthood.

So in that messy moment, I began to thank God for Ian and for the opportunity to give him what I never had. Even though I was still grossed out by Ian's explosive poop, I thanked God for a digestive system that worked properly. Although my son seemed to poop more powerfully than the average child, I was grateful that he was healthy and had a bright future in front of him.

God shifted my perspective on dealing with crap that day, and I want to share a few things I've learned about messes.

1. MESSES AND LIFE ARE CONNECTED. IF YOU DON'T HAVE ANY MESSES, YOU PROBABLY AREN'T REALLY LIVING.

I know I'm not alone in hating messes. I believe that most of us spend a lot of time trying to avoid them. The problem with living that way is that we end up wasting time running from the inevitable. Proverbs 14:4 (TPT) says it like this:

> *The only clean stable is an empty stable. So if you want the work of an ox and to enjoy an abundant harvest, you'll have a mess or two to clean up!*

In a culture that revolved around agriculture, oxen were animals used to produce crops that were needed to survive, make a profit, and contribute to society. This Scripture is saying that a farmer's stable would be cleaner without oxen, but he also wouldn't be able to do his job! In the same way, your life would be cleaner if you didn't have to deal with other people's crap – or your own – but if there aren't any messes, you probably aren't pursuing anything worthwhile.

In my life, planting a church was messy. We didn't know what we were doing and had no blueprints to follow. We made just as many messes as we had successes, but without the messes, the successes wouldn't have happened!

Relationships are usually messy, but finding a spouse to spend the rest of your life with is worth it. Following your dreams might be messy, but fulfilling your God-given destiny is worth it. When asking the Holy Spirit to help you overcome sin, you might mess up along the way, but the pursuit of freedom is worth it.

I fear that rather than finding meaning in our messes, we simply try to run from them. Once we find that we can't avoid them, we just complain about them. Yes, messes happen. No, they aren't fun. However, we can choose to accept them, find value in them, and grow from them, realizing that we'll never find success without some mess.

2. GOD VIEWS MESSES AS OPPORTUNITIES FOR MIRACLES.

Without a mess, there is no miracle. I know that's probably not what you want to hear. It would be awesome if we could have only miracles and no messes. I'd love to live a life where only good things ever take place and no bad things happen.

As great as that would be, it's a flawed way of thinking. Consider this for a second: if nothing bad ever happened, how would we be able to recognize and appreciate what is really good? It's the same way with messes. If they didn't exist, how would we be able to recognize and appreciate the miracles that God does in and through our lives?

According to the dictionary, the definition of a miracle is as follows: "an extraordinary event manifesting divine intervention in human affairs."[2]

Here's my translation: a miracle happens when, in the natural course of your daily life, God shows up and intervenes supernaturally. It's when he comes and changes everything in a way that only he could. But we wouldn't need a miracle unless there was a reason God needed to intervene. In order for there to be a miracle, there first has to be a mess!

WITH NO MESS THERE'S NO MIRACLE

We look at our messes the way that I first looked at Ian when he was blowing out his diapers. We get discouraged and frustrated. But God doesn't see things the way that you see them. God looks at the same mess and says, "This is an opportunity for me to intervene! I'm about to do a miracle and show everybody who I am."

The Bible is full of God showing up and doing miracles. What you'll find is that most of those miracles started as messes.

In the book of Exodus, the Israelites, God's chosen people, were enslaved to the Egyptians for 400 years. God appointed a man named Moses to free them from their bondage but the Egyptians didn't let the Israelites go easily. God sent ten plagues on Egypt, including things like infesting their country with frogs and sending locust to eat all of their crops. By the end of the tenth plague, the Egyptians had finally had enough. They decided to release God's people to freedom.

Once the Israelites escaped Egypt, they start to make their way to the Promised Land. All seemed to be going well until Pharaoh, the leader of Egypt, changed his mind about freeing the Israelites and decided to send his army after them. When the Israelites realized the Egyptians were pursuing them, they were on the shores of the Red Sea with no place to run. They became very angry and felt betrayed by God. It seemed he led them into the middle of a mess. In Exodus 14:10-12, they start yelling at the Lord and Moses, saying:

"Why did you bring us out here in the wilderness?

Weren't there enough graves for us in Egypt? What have you done to us? Why did you make us leave Egypt? Didn't we tell you this would happen while we were still in Egypt?"

Sound familiar? In the middle of a mess, the first thing they did was complain. They were mad at God and blaming Moses for getting them into this mess.

Remember when I said that God views a mess as an opportunity for a miracle? The Israelites only saw the mess, but God saw the opportunity.

God instructed Moses to pick up his staff and raise his hands over the Red Sea. As he did, the sea split in two, creating a strip of dry land for the Israelites to cross. The Egyptians chased them on the dry land, but as soon as the Israelites safely reached the other shore, the waters crashed back down, and engulfed the Egyptians!

When the people of Israel saw the mighty power that the Lord had unleashed against the Egyptians, they were filled with awe before him. They put their faith in the Lord and in their servant Moses.[3]

They experienced a miracle that not only delivered them from slavery but changed their perception of God forever. When God does any miracle in your life, he wants it to draw you into a closer relationship with him. He wants to develop your faith in such a way that it changes how you go on to live in the future.

Whenever you see a mess, God is inviting you to get

excited. The presence of a mess is an indication that some sort of miracle might be on its way – a miracle that shows you, and everyone else around you, who God really is.

———

So what should you do when you're in the middle of a mess? Before we end this chapter, I want to give you a few action steps that you can take right now.

1. ACKNOWLEDGE GOD IN THE MIDDLE OF YOUR MESS.

God has a lot to say in his Word about sticking by your side. He promises to be with you always, in any and every situation.

> *Be strong and courageous... The Lord himself goes before you and will be with you; he will never leave you nor forsake you. Do not be afraid; do not be discouraged. (Deuteronomy 31:7-8 NIV)*

> *Can anyone hide from me in a secret place? Am I not everywhere in all the heavens and earth? (Jeremiah 23:24)*

> *When you're in over your head, I'll be there with you. When you're in rough waters, you will not go down. When you're between a rock and a hard place, it won't be a dead end—Because I am God...*

So don't be afraid: I'm with you. (Isaiah 43:2-5 MSG)

And never forget that I am with you every day, even to the completion of this age. (Matthew 20:28 TPT)

It's clear that God doesn't leave, regardless of the mess that we are in – even if it's a mess we made ourselves! In the middle of your mess, it's easy to feel like God has abandoned you, but it's not true. Whether you feel it or not, God is right in the middle of your mess with you. When you acknowledge his presence, you gain access to the grace, wisdom, strength, and provision that you need.

2. WORSHIP IN THE MIDDLE OF YOUR MESS.

One night when Steph was leading worship at our church, she encouraged those in attendance with a statement that has always stuck with me. She said this:

SOMETIMES WE WORSHIP BECAUSE WE KNOW GOD IS GOOD, BUT SOMETIMES WE WORSHIP *UNTIL* WE KNOW HE'S GOOD.[4]

When we're in a situation that feels hopeless or messy, we need to remind ourselves that God is still in control, that he is still good. Worship elevates God to a position above ourselves, putting him back in his proper place. Worship shifts our perspective. Any time we take our eyes off of our own problems and focus them on Jesus, he lifts the heavy burdens that we have been carrying.

Yet it's often in the middle of a mess that we don't want to worship God. Our financial crisis or failing health might make us feel like we have no reason to thank God. The mistakes we continue to make might make us feel like we aren't worthy of being in God's presence. However, when we least feel like worshiping God is actually when we need to worship him most.

The point that Steph was making to our church is the same point that I'm trying to make to you – worshiping when you don't feel like it is what leads to freedom, joy, and confidence that God is faithful. Stop focusing on how big your mess is and start focusing on how big God is. If you can worship until you know God is good, the burden of your mess will be outweighed by the belief that God will bring you through it.

3. DEAL WITH YOUR OWN CRAP.

Remember when we explained that Bartimaeus was sitting by the wayside, i.e., the waste-side, i.e., sitting in crap? Any time we come face to face with the crap in our lives, God is giving us an invitation to evaluate how we got there. Sometimes messes just happen, but many messes in life are ones we create. Sin, poor decisions, or not listening to spiritual authority can produce messes.

As you've gathered from this entire chapter, God can show up and perform a miracle in the middle of your mess, but if the mess is self-made, he will also invite you to grow so you don't find yourself back there again. God can instantaneously deliver you, but will often guide you through a process of obedience to teach you how to live, so you don't keep making messes for yourself and everyone around you. Sometimes the miracles God does are activated through the process of learning to live according to his ways instead of your own.

Psalm 139:23-24 says,

> *Search me, O God, and know my heart; test me and know my anxious thoughts. Point out anything in me that offends you, and lead me along the path of everlasting life.*

Asking God to search your heart and point out anything that offends him is one of the most difficult prayers to pray. It's hard to acknowledge that we are probably doing more things that don't line up with God's heart than we realize. However, the most difficult things to do are typically the most transformative things we can do.

God doesn't get mad at you for getting yourself into a mess, but just as a good father brings correction to his children, God will bring correction to you. The Bible tells us:

> *Don't underestimate the value of the discipline and training of the Lord God, or get depressed when he has to correct you. For the Lord's training of your life is the evidence of his faithful love.[5]*

Many people think God wants to keep us from sin to

steal our fun, but that's far from the truth.

GOD DOESN'T WANT TO STEAL YOUR FUN, HE WANTS TO SAVE YOUR FUTURE.

He knows what is best for your life, and he can't stand to see you settle for anything less. It's out of his love for you, not anger towards you, that he challenges you to deal with your crap and get it cleaned up.

My prayer is that after this chapter you can start to look at messes differently. Bartimaeus was surrounded by a mess, but as you will soon find out, his mess became his message.

If you're stuck by the wayside, you don't have to stay there. God can change your perspective, help you deal with your crap, and redeem every moment. One day you'll be able to look back on that mess, celebrate the miracle that God did, and use it as a message to help transform someone else!

TWO
REFLECTION+APPLICATION

What messes have you been complaining about that you need to start thanking God for instead?

_____

_____

_____

_____

What's a time in your life when God turned your mess into a miracle? Acknowledge that he has the power to do the same thing in your current situation.

_____

_____

_____

_____

What crap do you need to deal with in your life? Ask the Holy Spirit to search your heart and help you overcome the things that have produced messes.

_____

_____

_____

_____

CHAPTER THREE

ONE WORD

WHEN BARTIMAEUS HEARD THAT JESUS OF NAZARETH WAS NEARBY, HE BEGAN TO SHOUT, "JESUS, SON OF DAVID, HAVE MERCY ON ME!"

MARK 10:47

When my oldest son, Parker, was getting ready to start kindergarten, he unintentionally taught me a powerful lesson about life.

One day my wife, wanting to start preparing our son for this transition, asked him, "Parker, are you excited about going to kindergarten?"

Parker got super excited. He responded, "YES! I can't wait to go to kindergarten!!"

At this point in his life, Parker was a pretty soft-spoken kid. We frequently had to encourage him to speak up because we couldn't understand what he was saying. He tended to use hand motions and whispers more than actual words. So, when Parker got excited and started screaming about going to kindergarten, Steph was surprised.

She asked what it was about kindergarten that made him so excited. He answered, "I can't wait to eat the Italian Classic!"

Now Steph was confused. "Parker, what are you talking about? You think that you're going to eat the Italian Classic at kindergarten? Where did you hear that?"

Parker persisted with even more passion, "YES! I can't wait. I want to go to kindergarten so we can have Italian Classic and giant MEATBALLS! I saw it on TV!"

My wife has a motherly gift of being able to understand our children and their gibberish better than anybody else. As she was listening to Parker rant and rave about the Italian Classic and kindergarten, she began to put two and two together.

At that time, I had been watching the NBA Finals most nights. Parker had been laying on the couch next to me and falling asleep during the games. Most of the time, I would tune out during the commercials, but I guess that's when Parker would tune in.

Steph thought back to some of the commercials that Parker had seen. As he was going on and on about the Italian Classic in kindergarten, she asked, "Parker, do you mean that you want to go to *Olive* Garden?"

"YES," he exclaimed, "Kinder Garden! The home of the world's largest meatball!"

My child was not used to commercials and didn't understand the goal behind them. He didn't know anything about marketing or advertising. He had no idea that their purpose is to convince you to buy the thing that they are trying to sell. We know that sometimes commercials stretch the truth, but Parker took all of the commercials at face value. He one hundred percent believed everything they had to say.

All of the commercials that we had watched for Olive Garden said that they had the world's largest meatball and encouraged customers to experience all the Italian classics. For you movie buffs out there, it reminded me of the scene in *Elf* when Buddy ran into a coffee shop and congratulated them for having "the world's best cup of coffee," as their advertisement board proclaimed. My five-year-old was like Buddy the Elf in this moment!

It's funny, for a minute we thought we had done an amazing job raising our son to be that excited to start kindergarten. We couldn't believe that he was so passionate about education at such a young age.

As it turns out, Parker could care less about going to kindergarten, but he was super passionate about going to Olive Garden. Who needs to learn the ABCs when you can be indulging on the Italian Classics?!

My point is this…

THERE IS POWER IN ONE WORD.

For Parker, the difference of one word had him thinking that we were going to take him to Olive Garden when we were actually going to drop him off at kindergarten. One word changed his entire reality.

As we dive further into the story of Bartimaeus, we find that his use of one word had the power to change everything for him.

SON OF DAVID

Even though Bartimaeus couldn't see, he could hear. As Jesus approached the wayside, I'm sure that Bartimaeus heard the hustle and bustle of the crowd. When he was told it was Jesus passing by, in the middle of the commotion, he shouted out.

"Jesus, Son of David, have mercy on me!"

It was a desperate moment for Bartimaeus. News of the miracles of Jesus had been spreading like wildfire throughout the region. Jesus had developed a reputation for healing sickness and disease. Blind eyes and deaf ears opened when he came around. It was even rumored that he had brought the dead back to life. And now that Jesus was so close to where Bartimaeus sat in his mess, he had an opportunity for his own miracle.

The way he addressed Jesus is very interesting–remember, one word can change everything. In that culture, people were typically identified by the name of their father or their hometown. Most people at that time would have called Jesus either "Jesus of Nazareth" or "Jesus, son of Joseph." Nazareth was the town where Jesus grew up. Joseph was the husband of Mary, Jesus' mother, and the man who raised him.

On the surface, the fact that Bartimaeus referred to Jesus as "Son of David" actually didn't make much sense. The question is why would he do it?

Stick with me for a second as we dive into a little bit of theology. Even though Joseph raised Jesus, he wasn't

Jesus' biological father. Jesus is God's Son. He came from Heaven to Earth in the form of a baby boy, conceived by the Holy Spirit through Mary, who was a virgin. Therefore, Jesus has a biological mother but is the only man in history to not have a true biological father. He was birthed through immaculate conception.

People referred to Jesus as the son of Joseph because they didn't believe or had no clue that he was the Son of God. Therefore, those who referred to him as "Jesus of Nazareth" or "Jesus, son of Joseph," thought that he was just another ordinary guy. Some recognized that he was a great teacher or powerful miracle worker, but they didn't recognize him as God in human flesh living among them.

At this time, the Jews held on to God's promise that a Messiah was coming. Many Israelites believed this meant that the Messiah would save them from the Roman oppression they were living under and overthrow the government. However, God had bigger plans and sent Jesus to save the world from sin and offer eternal life. Even though their Savior had arrived, most didn't realize it.

The Old Testament prophets, those appointed by God to speak his words and deliver his messages to the world, had foretold that God would send someone to save his people. There are many prophecies stating things like what town the Messiah would come from, that he would be born to a virgin, how people would respond to him, and ultimately that he would die as a perfect sacrifice for sin. There were also specific prophecies that stated the

Savior would come from the family line of David, the greatest King in the history of Israel.[1]

I hope you're still with me because here's where it gets good! When Bartimaeus called Jesus the "Son of David," he was acknowledging what God's prophets had said about the coming Savior. He believed that Jesus wasn't just a son of Joseph, but that he was from the family line of King David – that he was the promised Messiah! My interpretation of that one little word-change says something like this:

> "Jesus, I believe you aren't just another man, but rather the Son of God. You're the Savior who came to change everything for us. You're not just a teacher or a miracle worker, you're our King, our God!"

Bartimaeus approached Jesus by calling him the "Son of David" rather than the "son of Joseph" and that one word changed everything! What you have to get is this:

THE WAY WE APPROACH JESUS CAN PUSH US CLOSER TO OR FURTHER AWAY FROM OUR MIRACLE.

Bartimaeus could have approached Jesus like most others did, believing that even though he did special things, he wasn't *that* special. He was only Joseph's son, and Joseph was an ordinary man. He was stuck in the middle class and had to work hard to make a living. How could a carpenter's son from Nazareth be the Messiah?

However, Bartimaeus didn't approach Jesus the way most others did. Whatever he had heard about Jesus up to that point caused him to believe that Jesus was not just a carpenter's son, he was the Son of God. A carpenter's son wouldn't have supernatural ability, but the Son of God would have the ability to not only forgive sins but also to give sight to the blind.

Bartimaeus referred to Jesus as the Son of David and made a request that only the Son of God has the power to grant. "Have mercy on me!" he pleaded. He asked for mercy because he knew who Jesus was. He understood that mercy was what he was all about.

We'll discover Jesus' response to the cry of Bartimaeus in a few pages. But first I have a question for you:

HOW DO YOU APPROACH JESUS?

If you approach Jesus strictly as a historical figure, chances are you'll never experience the mercy that he wants to offer you.

If you approach Jesus believing that he was a great teacher, good advice is about as much as you're going to get out of him.

If you approach Jesus as someone who is only relevant for other people, you most likely won't experience his transformative power.

However, if you approach Jesus as the Savior, he has the power to free you from your sin and lead you to eternal life as you put your faith in him.

If you approach him as the one who sits in Heaven with the world as his footstool,[2] then he can bring his posture of peace to your crazy world.

If you approach Jesus as the one who was wounded so you could be whole,[3] he can bring healing to your body, relationships, and situations.

If you approach him as the one who is seated at the right hand of the Father advocating for you,[4] you can live with confidence knowing that he is fighting on your behalf.

If you approach Jesus believing that he understands your weaknesses and faced all the same tests you face, yet overcame them, then you can "come boldly to the throne of our gracious God. There we will receive his mercy, and we will find grace to help us when we need it most."[5]

Remember this: the "word" that you use to approach Jesus can change your reality. You might not always need a miracle but you will always need mercy.

THE WAY YOU APPROACH JESUS WILL DETERMINE WHAT YOU RECEIVE FROM HIM.

Before we end this chapter, I want to give you some practical advice about approaching Jesus. As we've already discussed, the foundation of our approach to Jesus should be the understanding that he is God. With that in mind, there are a few specific ways to approach God that will help us fully experience him and his power in our lives.

YOU MIGHT NOT ALWAYS NEED A MIRACLE BUT YOU WILL ALWAYS NEED MERCY

PRIDE VS HUMILITY

Pride is defined as "a high or inordinate opinion of one's own dignity, importance, merit, or superiority."[6] Pride is the idea that you are the central figure in your life. You are the one who makes things happen. Pride assumes that if anything good comes along it's because of your own ability. Pride prohibits God's power.

God showing up and moving in my life is all about his mercy, not my ability. For God's power to start working, my power has to stop. God's power is activated by permission, and giving God permission to do what he wants instead of what I want requires humility.

Humility means "having a modest opinion or estimate of one's own importance."[7] Humility isn't thinking lowly of yourself; rather, it's realizing that you have limitations. It's only when you become aware of your limitations that you recognize your need for God's limitless power. God's help is activated by humility.

When Jesus showed up on the scene, Bartimaeus approached him with a humble heart. If Bartimaeus thought that he had his situation under control, he would not have called out to Jesus. If Bartimaeus had the power to change his condition, surely he would have already done so. Living blind for his entire life, Bartimaeus was acutely aware of his own limitations. He knew that his only hope for a miracle was divine intervention.

ARE YOU APPROACHING GOD WITH PRIDE OR HUMILITY?

SOMEONE WHO HAS A PRIDEFUL APPROACH:

» Doesn't spend much time in prayer
» Tries to control every detail of life
» Has a hard time admitting when they're wrong
» Believes they are good at everything
» Takes all credit for the success they've had
» Doesn't ask for help often
» Doesn't value the advice of mentors, coaches, or pastors

SOMEONE WHO HAS A HUMBLE APPROACH:

» Prays often, even about small things
» Trusts God when things don't make sense
» Will own part of the blame, even if they're mostly right
» Recognizes their weaknesses
» Gives credit to God and others when they succeed
» Realizes they are stronger with the help of God and others
» Applies the advice mentors, coaches, or pastors give

James 4:6 is a perfect example of how pride and humility affect our interactions with God:

God opposes the proud, but gives grace to the humble.

In the original Greek, the word "oppose," *antitássomai*, is an old military term that was used to describe an officer placing his soldiers in position to attack an enemy. In other words, when you are prideful, you set yourself up as an enemy of what God wants to do in your life. Because he can't work with you, he must set himself up against you. But God's heart is not to oppose you, it's to fight for you!

I look at the second half of James 4:6 as an invitation. If you're willing to humble yourself, God will give you grace – he'll lift you up, he'll empower you, he'll work on your behalf. When you approach God with humility, you'll be in the right position to see his goodness and receive his mercy.

SAVIOR VS GOD

When I first gave my life to Jesus, my Uncle Dave gave me a bunch of Christian CDs. One of them was by the band Jars of Clay (hopefully, we have some mid-nineties Christian music fans reading this)! One of my favorite songs from their album was "Love Song for a Savior," and one particular line in that song has stuck with me to this day:

It seems too easy to call You Savior
Not close enough to call You God [8]

For the longest time, I couldn't understand what that lyric meant. As my relationship with Jesus continued to grow deeper, one day it finally hit me.

Many of us call out to Jesus in a moment that we need to be saved. It's easy to do that! When we've hit rock bottom, reached the end our rope, when the crap's hit the fan, when there's nowhere else to turn – then we cry out to God. It's as if we are on a life raft in the middle of the ocean and he is the rescue boat that's zipping past.

There's nothing wrong with calling out to Jesus in those moments; in fact, he wants us to call on him to save us! However, if those are the *only* moments we cry out for Jesus, we are missing a huge part of the close relationship he desires to have with us. He doesn't just want to be your Savior, he wants to be your God.

Sometimes we scream, "Jesus, save me!" but then we fail to stay connected to him after the rescue. He gets us out of our mess, and we say "k thanks bye" until the next time we need help.

ASKING JESUS TO BE SAVIOR GIVES HIM ACCESS TO BE YOUR LIFELINE, BUT ALLOWING HIM TO BE GOD GIVES HIM FULL ACCESS TO YOUR LIFE.

As we continue to read the story of Bartimaeus, you will see that he never turns to anybody else; he fixes his focus on Jesus for his salvation and healing, but also for his future. He gives Jesus complete control.

Jesus wants us to give him complete control of our lives. He wants us to call out to him not only when we need to be saved, but also in the course of everyday life. He wants us to trust him not only when things are falling apart but also when they are going well. He wants us to be obedient even when our personal preference isn't necessarily what his Word says.

God can give you a miracle in the middle of your emergency, but how many miracles might we miss if we only go to him when there is an emergency? God will show you mercy in the middle of your mess, but if you only ever ask him to clean up your messes, how much of who God is will you never see? The Bible says his love and mercy are new every morning.[9] God wants to do extraordinary things in your life every single day, but to do that, he must have access.

I want to challenge you to not only make Jesus your Savior but understand that he also needs to be your God. One word in Bartimaeus' approach to Jesus led to his miracle. I believe that one word in your approach can lead to yours.

Whatever situation or circumstance you are facing right now, you can approach Jesus in the same way that Bartimaeus did – acknowledge him as God and humbly ask for mercy. You have the power to pray a prayer that can change your reality:

JESUS, SON OF DAVID, HAVE MERCY ON ME...

THREE

REFLECTION + APPLICATION

Do you believe that Jesus is the Son of God? If not, ask him to reveal who he is to you!

_____

_____

_____

Do you have more qualities of a prideful person or humble person? What attitudes might you need to adjust to approach God the right way?

_____

_____

_____

Do you only call on Jesus when you need help or does he have full control of your life? What's the first step that you can take to give him more access to you?

_____

_____

_____

Think of an area of your life in which you need a miracle. Ask for Jesus to show you mercy. Acknowledge that it's only through his power that anything can change!

_____

_____

_____

CHAPTER FOUR

HATERS OR ELEVATORS

"BE QUIET!" MANY OF THE PEOPLE YELLED AT HIM.

MARK 10:48

This chapter is all about one thing – HATERS!

If you read my first book, *Notorious*, you might remember that I talked about haters in it as well. I hate to sound like a broken record, but the longer I serve Jesus, the more I find it is something that continuously comes up. What I'm starting to realize is that no matter what you do, you'll always have haters. Jesus had to deal with them, I've had to navigate them, and you'll have to face them as well.

How would you define a hater?

In the context of pursuing the will of God for your life, a hater cannot simply be defined as somebody who doesn't like you. Everyone has people who don't like them. Haters are people who come against what God is doing in your life. It could be because of jealousy, self-righteousness, lack of understanding, or disagreement with what you're doing. I'm convinced that sometimes people hate on you simply because they are miserable and have nothing else to do!

You can't always put your finger on exactly why haters do what they do – haters gonna hate, right? However, the thing that seems to be true more often than not is that the very presence of haters in your life has spiritual significance attached to it. For whatever reason, when God is working in and through you, haters appear.

This not a concept unique to the 21st century. We can even find haters in the story of Bartimaeus over 2,000 years ago...

HATERS OR ELEVATORS

Bartimaeus was finally about to have an encounter with Jesus. It seemed like he'd been waiting his entire life for this moment. Every single day, he lived the reality of being a blind beggar – separated from everyone else, unable to do the things everyone else did – and now the One who was opening blind eyes was so close. He shouted out for Jesus!

When I read stories in the Bible, I sometimes like to think of what *should* have happened. Often, it's not until we have an understanding of what should have happened that we can learn from what actually happened. I would like to think that the people of Jericho would have been happy for Bartimaeus to get his moment with Jesus. They must have walked by him many times, begging for a living by the wayside, and maybe tossed him a shekel once or twice. He had a tough go at life and this was his chance to be able to see! They could look forward to watching the testimony video at church on Sunday and shedding a few tears.

Maybe that's what should have happened, but that's not what actually happened. Instead, in response to Bartimaeus shouting for Jesus, people yelled at him:

"BE QUIET!"

It's frustrating when you read it. Why should they care if Bartimaeus got a miracle? Why would they try to prevent him from pursuing Jesus? Maybe they were just consumed with their own agendas, or maybe it was something more.

In Jewish culture, people were led by religious leaders who were exactly what that title says they were: religious. God had given the Israelites 613 commandments to follow so they could prosper and live in peace with him and each other. The laws revolved around things like morality and the proper way to have religious ceremonies, and were intended to serve as guidelines to ultimately keep the people turned toward God and his love.

Jewish leaders were obsessed with the Law. They not only taught all 613, but they also added complicated layers onto the existing regulations. Tons of new rules were created to try to clarify the already existing commandments. If it wasn't already hard enough to experience God, they made it harder.

Jesus was in constant conflict with the Jewish religious leaders, especially the sect called Pharisees. He wasn't impressed with their knowledge of the Law or their obsession to appear perfect. The Law was intended to draw and keep people's hearts close to God, but the religious leaders never got that! In Matthew 23, Jesus has a field day calling them out. Before roasts became popular on late-night television, Jesus roasted the Pharisees:

> *"What sorrow awaits you teachers of religious law and you Pharisees. Hypocrites! For you are so careful to clean the outside of the cup and the dish, but inside you are filthy—full of greed and self-indulgence! You blind Pharisee! First wash the inside of the cup and the dish, and then the outside will become clean, too."[1]*

In other words, the Pharisee's main concern was to look good on the outside. They wanted to appear as if they followed all of the rules, lived perfectly, and had it all together, yet their hearts were far from God. They couldn't admit their need for God's mercy. They thought they could obtain his blessings through their own efforts. Not only did they get it wrong, but they made it more difficult for everybody else with their self-imposed, man-made additions to the Law. They expected people to be perfect and never extended the love or grace of God to them.

When Bartimaeus called out for Jesus, he did so in the middle of a highly religious culture. People had been taught that perfection was what attracted God's blessing. There was no room for sin, mistakes, impairments, sickness, or disease. If you weren't perfect, you had better cover it up and pretend like you were.

When people looked at Bartimaeus, they saw the opposite of perfection. They saw imperfection at its finest. He was blind. He was a beggar. He was sitting in sewage. I'm sure they thought he did something to earn that lot in life, assuming it was punishment for some type of sin. And Bartimaeus wasn't even trying to cover it up. There he was, yelling at the top of his lungs, his shame on display for everyone to see – for *Jesus* to see.

Much of the crowd that surrounded Jesus likely believed that such a godly teacher wouldn't want to be bothered by this lowly outcast. A blind beggar surely wasn't worthy. But that didn't stop Bartimaeus from yelling. And that didn't sit right with the people's religious attitudes. In fact, it offended them.

Any time you do something that offends religious people, you can be certain some haters will be birthed. So even though Bartimaeus was pursuing God's best for his life, he developed haters who were trying to stop him.

Do you remember from the last chapter that we can approach God with either pride or humility? The haters trying to silence Bartimaeus were prideful, thinking that you had to have it all together to get God's attention. But Bartimaeus was humble, acknowledging that he didn't have it all together and was desperate for a miracle.

According to God's Word, the haters were in the wrong, and Bartimaeus was the one doing it right. In other words, sometimes we experience opposition, not when we're doing things wrong, but because we're doing things right. In fact, the more closely you follow the plans Jesus has for you, the more opposition you will encounter.

Some of you reading this have already experienced some haters in your spiritual journey. Maybe as you've made steps to pursue your purpose, people have told you to slow down or stop. Maybe when you've shared your God-sized dreams, they've said that you're being unrealistic. Maybe as you've grown in passion, people have told you that you look obnoxious. Maybe as you've grown in generosity, people have said that you're giving too much of yourself to the church and others. Maybe as you've been trying to love and serve the world around you, they've said you don't have the right motives and are doing it for your own glory.

I know that the opposition you are experiencing hurts. Believe me, I've felt that hurt and if I could prevent it, for both of us, I would. However, there is some good news: if you're pursuing Jesus and religious people are offended by what you are doing, it's a good indicator that you're on the right path.

Most of the time, we think that haters are indicators that we should stop, but haters are actually indicators that we should continue heading in the direction that we are going.

Haters serve as the gatekeepers to your future.

Haters are elevators.

When you experience new devils, you are about to graduate to a new level.

When you experience hate, you get to choose how

you respond. The pain that you experience has the power to stop you or to propel you. 1 Peter 4:19 (TPT) says,

> *Those who suffer for following God's will should enfold their lives into the Creator, who will never fail them, and continue to always do what is right.*

You can give up because it hurts, or you can take that hurt to Jesus. Opposition can lead you to a level of intimacy with God that you've never experienced before. And I believe the further your roots grow down into intimacy, the more fruit your life will produce.

In the story of Joseph in the book of Genesis, when Joseph's brothers apologize for selling him into slavery (and you thought you had sibling rivalry!), Joseph has an amazing response that says a lot about how God can use opposition and hate in our lives.

Joseph had become the second-hand man to Pharaoh, the ruler of all Egypt. He was in the process of saving entire countries from a drought. However, he wouldn't have been in position to do any of this if his brothers hadn't sold him as a slave. Joseph says in Genesis 50:20, "You intended to harm me, but God intended it all for good. He brought me to this position so I could save the lives of many people."

WHAT OTHER PEOPLE MEANT TO HURT YOU, GOD CAN USE TO HELP YOU.

What was meant to tear you down can actually serve

to lift you up to your purpose. If you've currently been dealing with haters, instead of being discouraged, be encouraged. God is getting ready to propel you into a new season!

CHRISTIAN CRITICS

I've had my fair share of what I like to call "Christian Critics" since we've planted Rust City Church. It was shocking to me that other Christians would try to attack and stop what God was so evidently doing. We were seeing people come to Jesus for the first time; we were witnessing the Holy Spirit transform lives. I expected hate from atheists or people who rejected church, but to my surprise, most of the hate we received came from other Christians.

People have visited our church just to let us know how ungodly we are. We've been bombarded by negative and slanderous social media posts. There have been videos and blogs created specifically to come against me as a pastor.

I'm not sharing this with you as some sort of badge of honor that I wear. Trust me, I do not enjoy receiving criticism. My natural desire is to be a people-pleaser. Every personality test I've ever taken confirms that's who I am. I like everyone to be happy and get along, so when I find people angry with me over things that I don't even view as the most important parts of church, it hurts! Naturally, when I get hurt, I want to strike back. When I feel attacked, I want to fight back. And believe me, I can strike with a vengeance. I know that I have enough argumentative ammunition loaded up to be able to prove these haters wrong and even make them look stupid. In my flesh, I want to make them look stupid!

But time and time again, God whispers to my heart: "You do not need to fight these battles. I did not put you on this planet to argue with other Christians. Trust that I'm big enough to defend you."

Every time that I want to put critics in their place, God uses the same Scripture to put me in my place. Jesus says in Matthew 7:2 (NIV):

For in the same way you judge others, you will be judged, and with the measure you use, it will be measured to you.

That Scripture has the power to keep you up at night! It's very easy to judge someone for judging you, but then you're doing the same thing that you are angry at them for doing to you. If people choose to criticize me as I serve God, then they will have to answer for it themselves. But as soon as I choose to lay into them, now I have to answer!

My challenge for all of us is to not build our lives on the idea that we need to tear down other people. We also don't need to live our lives attacking those who attack us. Whether you're offended by something that somebody else is doing, or you're offended that somebody is offended by you, you can move past it.

We live in a culture where every person has a platform to voice their every opinion, and the media teaches us that if we disagree with something we have to hate the person who said it. I believe that God has put you on this planet for a purpose, but it isn't using your social media platform to tear others down.

God doesn't need you to tell every person you know how terrible somebody is just because you don't agree with them! He doesn't need you to be his watchdog and attack when you think someone's in the wrong. He doesn't need you to defend yourself or get into arguments for the world to see, especially with other Christians. When you do that, you not only make them look bad, you make yourself look bad. Often, you make Christianity and the church as a whole look bad! Who would want to be a part of a family that hates each other and fights all the time?

Even if there is something that concerns you about another person or ministry, the right response is not to go public. Instead, pray first, and then, if it's someone you know, talk to them privately.

God is not only all-powerful, he's also all-knowing. In his sovereignty and wisdom, he can sort things out if other churches or other people need correction. He can speak to them. He can use the accountability and authority he has placed in their lives to get ahold of them. There are times that God may ask you to speak the truth in love to those with whom you have influence (we will talk about that a little bit later in this chapter), but you have to realize that it is not your job to be God's watchdog for the whole world. You have to trust that he's got things under control.

Remember, Jesus said we will be judged by the same measure that we judge others. Others may not always be right, but I know that I'm not always right either. Even when I'm wrong, I'd hope that Jesus and others would approach me with grace. I'd hope they would think the best of me and believe that my heart is in the right place even if I'm making a few mistakes. That's what Love does: it doesn't demand its own way, it keeps no record of wrongs, it believes the best of others, it never fails.[2] It doesn't neglect the fact that I have things I need to change; however, I'm much more likely to change as I'm empowered by love and grace, not threatened by hate.

We have the opportunity to lead with love. We are invited to think the best of others rather than assume the worst. The same mercy that God extends to us when we don't deserve it, is the same mercy that we can extend to others. As we do, not only will other's receive his grace, but we will receive the same measure of it as well.

PICK YOUR FIGHT

I tend to think that the last words somebody speaks are their most important ones. If someone close to you knew they didn't have long to live, they would probably use their last conversations to share their heart for you in a deep way. They might tell you how they've always felt about you, encourage you, or give you guidance on how you should live based on what they have learned.

This is the exact situation we find Jesus in during his

last moments on earth. Jesus had died for the sins of the world on the cross, risen from the grave, and was about to ascend to Heaven. For his followers, this was the last time they would experience Jesus in physical form. It was a monumental moment during which they would cling to the words that he spoke. Jesus could have encouraged them with anything, and here's what he chose:

> *"But you will receive power when the Holy Spirit comes upon you. And you will be my witnesses, telling people about me everywhere—in Jerusalem, throughout Judea, in Samaria, and to the ends of the earth." After saying this, he was taken up into a cloud while they were watching, and they could no longer see him.[3]*

As we've already discussed, Jesus dealt with a lot of haters during his time on earth. The religious leaders constantly attacked him, his ministry, and even plotted to kill him! He knew that the disciples would receive the same type of hate. Before going to the cross, Jesus told them in John 15:18-19,

> *"If the world hates you, remember that it hated me first. The world would love you as one of its own if you belonged to it, but you are no longer part of the world. I chose you to come out of the world, so it hates you."*

Jesus knew that his followers would not just face

opposition, but persecution. However, with his very last words, he didn't encourage them to clap back at those who criticized them. He didn't teach self-defense tactics to deploy against religious people. Rather, Jesus simply told his followers to tell people everywhere about him. He empowered them to take the Good News to the ends of the earth.

Jesus knew that when they did, they would receive hate. As you seek to follow Jesus' final words, he knows that it's going to be a battle. Yet, he gave us a laser-focused command on what we should put our energy toward: helping those who are far from God find him.

Christianity will inevitably be a fight. My question for you is this: Which fight will you choose?

WILL YOU CHOOSE TO FIGHT *AGAINST* CHRISTIAN CRITICS OR WILL YOU FIGHT *FOR* THOSE WHO ARE FAR FROM GOD?

Let's talk about professional fighting for a second. Before two boxers fight, they have to agree to a contract. They take into consideration the rank of their opponent, the revenue the match will generate, the terms and location of the fight, the popularity it will bring, and how much each boxer has to lose.

One of the most anticipated fights in boxing history happened in 2015 when Floyd "Money" Mayweather took on Manny Pacquiao. Mayweather was an undefeated, five-division world champion and Pacquiao was an eight-division world champion. The boxing world had pushed for this fight to happen as early as 2009, but neither side agreed to fight until 2015. For seven years, the two boxers chose not to fight. At the time, it wasn't worth it for them. When they finally matched up, it was the highest-grossing pay-per-view fight in history, bringing in a revenue of over $410 million.[4]

In the same way, you get to pick your fights. Not every fight is worth it. You only have so much energy as a human being. You only have so much time. Do you want to spend it fighting pointless battles or do you want to fight the *good* fight?[5] I want to encourage you to follow the commands of Jesus, and as you do, watch how God fights for you. As you put your focus on loving instead of hating those whom God loves, you'll inevitably find the victory that Jesus has already won.

ACCOUNTABILITY VS CRITICISM

As we talk about things like judgment and criticism, I want to give you a quick disclaimer. I want to make sure that you don't misinterpret the heart of what I'm trying to say. I'm not saying that there isn't a very clear standard in the Bible on how we should aim to live. There are many things that the Bible defines as sin. I believe that as followers of Jesus, through the power of the Holy Spirit, we can live sin-free lives as we learn to walk in the freedom that is available to us. I don't believe that any of us are exempt from judgment or are above people speaking into our lives.

For example, there are many specific instructions in the Bible on how I, as a pastor, should live my life. 1 Timothy 3:1-7 details that a church leader should be above reproach, faithful to his wife, self-controlled, not quarrelsome, not greedy, and more. I don't take that lightly! There are also verses on how you should live with integrity if you want to serve and have influence in the church.[6] And even if you're not a church leader, the Bible is *full* of instruction on how to live a godly life.

Of course, none of us are perfect; we definitely don't get it right all the time. But Jesus wants our hearts in a position to desire and chase after the lifestyle that he laid out. That's why it's important to listen to accountability in your life!

There are people God has placed in my life who have the right to call me out on my crap. They have the freedom to tell me when I'm missing the mark or making poor decisions. Accountability is healthy and necessary. It's one of the things that God uses to keep our hearts in the right place as we pursue our purpose.

One of my favorite verses on accountability is found in the book of James. James 5:16 says,

> *Confess your sins to each other and pray for each other so that you may be healed.*

Accountability not only helps to keep us from sin, but it also leads to our healing.

However, there is a difference between accountability and criticism.

Accountability comes from people who have spiritual authority over you or permission to speak into your life. They should be godly people that you know and trust, so you can be confident that the correction and guidance you receive is rooted in love. Their desire is for you to discover God's best for your life.

Criticism comes from people who haven't been given access to speak into your life. They may have proximity but they don't have permission. They aren't privy to what's really going on behind the scenes in your life; they're just forming opinions based on their own perception. They could be religious people who just want things their way or offended people who are taking their offense out on you. Whatever the motive, their goal isn't to build you up but rather to tear you down.

Obviously, we can't stop ourselves from hearing what people say to us or about us, unless we act like a toddler, stick our fingers in our ears, and shout "LA-LA-LA, I CAN'T HEAR YOU." But when we do hear negative feedback, we can choose to let it in or let it go.

When you're deciding what words to receive and what words to reject, first consider what role the speaker has in your life. Second, ask yourself if this person is who you'd want to be.

RECEIVE FROM THOSE YOU WANT TO BE LIKE.

Never accept criticism from someone you wouldn't want to trade places with in life. For example, would you take marriage advice from somebody who has been divorced five times? No! You would seek out a couple with a successful, godly marriage. You'd trust the couple who have been married for fifty years and still love each other to know what they're talking about! My point is this: listen to those that you want to be like.

Most of the accountability in my life comes from pastors. Why? Because I'm a pastor! I've sought out friends and mentors who lead fruitful, life-giving churches. They've been doing this longer than I have. They've figured out how to have healthy relationships with Jesus and their families while leading healthy ministries. I let them challenge me and I accept their guidance, even when they tell me things I don't want to hear, because I want to be like them!

Unless God convicts me, I rarely receive criticism from negative or religious people on how to pastor. Nothing against them, but they've never done what I'm doing. They may not fully understand the tensions and challenges I'm experiencing. It doesn't mean that I shouldn't pray about some of the things they say. It's always a good idea to ask God to search your heart and make sure that it's in a good place, but if the Holy Spirit doesn't confirm the criticism, I let it go. I won't disregard the vision God has given me just to please someone else, especially if I wouldn't want to trade places with that person.

Stop listening to people you don't want to be like. Stop allowing criticism to cripple you. Instead, get some accountability in your life. Start learning from people you *do* want to be like. The more vulnerable you become with them, the more their wisdom will lead you to be the person God has called you to be.

THE MENTALITY OF JESUS

Before we end this chapter, I want to encourage you with an example of how Jesus handled haters. We've already touched on this, but if anybody was ever criticized, it was Jesus. He was a punching bag for people to verbally assault. That's why I try to not take criticism too seriously. Jesus, who had the purest motives and lived a totally perfect life, was accused of working for the devil![7]

In John 5, Jesus had the perfect mentality while taking intense criticism. He came upon a man who was lame for thirty-eight years and couldn't even stand up. After an encounter with Jesus, the man rolled up his mat and walked away! It was a miraculous moment that changed this man's life forever. However, the religious leaders (Christian critics) were upset that Jesus healed the man on the Sabbath. They viewed the miracle as "work," and Jewish Law decreed that no labor was to be done on that day.

They were so upset that they started to harass Jesus and began searching for ways to kill him. Jesus responded in John 5:19,

> *"I tell you the truth, the Son can do nothing by himself. He does only what he sees the Father doing. Whatever the Father does, the Son also does."*

In response to criticism, Jesus didn't second-guess himself or agree to stop doing miracles on the Sabbath because it upset some people. He didn't change his entire mission to please the critics. Rather, he reiterated whose direction he was following, who he cared about pleasing.

The main objective of Jesus was to please his Father. So much so that he "only did what he saw the Father do." Jesus walked in close connection to God the Father, listened intently to his voice, and trusted and obeyed his leadership. It wasn't that Jesus was purposefully trying to offend religious people, it's just that in fulfilling the Father's purpose, the religious people got offended. But the approval of the Father was more important to Jesus than the approval of man.

I'm not proposing that you should intentionally offend people. I'm letting you know, however, that when you walk with God like Jesus did, you're going to offend some people. In fulfilling your God-given purpose, there will be people who don't understand (God's ways are not our ways) and try to tear you down. In those moments, you have to remember why you're doing what you're doing.

ARE YOU DOING IT FOR HIM OR ARE YOU DOING IT FOR THEM?

Jesus should not only be your strength, he should also be your motivation. If your motives are right, your mentality can be right. And if your mentality is right, you can fulfill your God-ordained mission in the face of opposition.

When Bartimaeus shouted, his haters tried to stop him. By ignoring the haters and keeping his eyes focused on Jesus, he kept himself in the running for his miracle.

Bartimaeus wanted his sight to be restored. However, maybe just for this one moment, it was to his advantage that he couldn't see. Because he was blind to the world, he was also blind to the people who criticized him.

Do you need to become "blind" to those criticize you? Maybe you're so focused on what others are saying that you've lost focus on Jesus. Your ability to keep your eyes on him may be what leads to your breakthrough.

FOUR
REFLECTION + APPLICATION

Have you been hurt by haters? Invite God into the wounded areas of your life. Ask him to help you forgive the people who caused you pain.

_____

_____

_____

Have you been judgmental of others, talked about them behind their backs or posted about them on social media? Ask God to help you see them through his love.

_____

_____

_____

What can you do every week to focus on those who are far from God?

_____

_____

_____

Do you have accountability in your life? If not, find someone you want to be like and ask if they will speak into your life.

_____

_____

_____

CHAPTER FIVE

PUNCHED IN THE MOUTH

BUT HE ONLY
SHOUTED LOUDER.
"SON OF DAVID,
HAVE MERCY ON ME!"

MARK 10:48

Mike Tyson is arguably one of the biggest, baddest boxers of all time. In 1985, at the age of 18, he knocked out his opponent, Hector Mercedes, in the first round. From that point on, he never looked back. By age 20, Tyson had a record of 22-0. Out of his 22 wins, 21 of them came by knockout. Some of those knockouts were in record time. He became the youngest heavyweight champion of the world and went on to be the first person ever to own all three major boxing belts.[1]

Mike Tyson was a dude that you did not want to mess with.

Even so, one of Tyson's opponents decided to trash talk him before a match. He boasted that he was the better boxer, claiming Tyson was no match for his style, movement, and quickness. The competitor claimed that he had watched tape after tape of Tyson and had the perfect game plan to defeat him.

In the boxing world, it's the media's job to stir up controversy before a fight, pitting the boxers against each other for added drama, trying to make the fight personal. In a press conference, a reporter let Tyson know what his opponent had said. The reporter asked if there was any validity to "the perfect game plan" to finally defeat Mike Tyson, and prodded, "Mike, how do you respond?"

Mike Tyson looked at the reporter dead in the eyes. With cold-blooded confidence, he said, "Everybody has a plan until they get punched in the mouth."[2]

Mike Tyson may have been a little crazy – or totally crazy – and taken one too many blows to the head, but there is a lot of truth in what he said.

EVERYBODY HAS A PLAN UNTIL THEY GET PUNCHED IN THE MOUTH.

Anyone can make a plan, but not everyone responds well when things don't go according to that plan. Don't get me wrong, I think it's much better to have a plan than no plan at all. Most people without a plan don't accomplish much in life.

Maybe you plan to get out of debt, you want to start tithing, or you're saving money for a vacation. Maybe you plan to go back to school and get a degree, or pursue a new job or promotion. You might desire to grow spiritually. Maybe you're planning to read your Bible every day or start serving at church. Maybe you know you need to go to anger management or marriage counseling or enter a recovery program.

Those are all great plans. I'm glad you have a plan. But my question for you is this:

What do you do when things don't go according to plan? What do you do when you get punched in the face? How do you respond when something or someone is standing right in the middle of your plan, attempting to throw you off course?

Most people don't handle adversity well. But I've never accomplished anything that I've set out to do in my life without adversity. I bet you haven't either. It seems like as soon as you decide to tithe, save, or knock down your debt, an unexpected medical or car bill pops up. As soon as you decide to get your degree or work on your marriage, you'll immediately be reminded of all the hurdles you face. As soon as you start to pursue God more deeply, the devil will attack you more ferociously. When you start making progress in overcoming addictions, stronger temptation will come out of nowhere.

When adversity hits your life, how you respond will determine whether you win or lose. What you choose to do in the moment you get punched in the mouth will dictate whether or not the plans you made, or even the plans God gave you, succeed or fail.

———

Bartimaeus had a plan to get Jesus' attention. As I mentioned in the last chapter, when Bartimaeus found out Jesus was nearby, he began to envision his miracle. Perhaps he imagined seeing beautiful colors for the first time. Maybe he was thinking about finally getting out of all that waste and being able to take a bath. He knew he had to get to Jesus to receive his miracle, but first Bartimaeus had to make it past his haters. His haters stood in between him and his plans. He couldn't turn around and wait until later or find an alternate route. If he was going to experience everything that God had for his life, he had to go directly through them.

His haters served as his adversity. As soon as Bartimaeus tried to enact his plan, shouting to get Jesus' attention, people try to shut him up. Now, I know the text only records him calling out to Jesus two times, but I think he was probably a little more persistent than that. I doubt that shouting twice would have been enough, when he was sitting by the wayside, far from the main road with a large, noisy crowd of people between him and Jesus. He was probably shouting pretty obnoxiously – after all, he's desperate – and the haters gotta hate. "BE QUIET!" they said, implying, *you're not good enough for Jesus to stop, so just leave him alone.*

But when they told Bartimaeus to be quiet, what did he do? When he got his "punch in the mouth," when he was faced with a challenge, did he back down? No! He shouted LOUDER.

He didn't stop. He kept shouting.

Louder and louder:

**"JESUS! SON OF DAVID!
HAVE MERCY ON ME!"**

We know Bartimaeus had a crappy life as a blind beggar sitting in filth. With so much adversity already in his life, how much more can he take? But in the face of another challenge, when it looked like his plans might fall through, and when his one hope for a miracle to get him out of his mess was passing by, when everything was telling him to quit, Bartimaeus didn't give up. He only shouted louder.

SOMETIMES, GOD WILL ALLOW ADVERSITY IN YOUR LIFE TO SEE HOW YOU RESPOND.

Will you quit? Give up? Accept your fate?
Or will you shout louder? Fight harder?

Proverbs 19:21 says,

You can make many plans, but the Lord's purpose will prevail.

Sometimes our plans fall short of God's purpose. He's not always concerned with our short-term goals; he's planning our eternity. You might want to be healthy, happy, and successful, but God's purpose for you is so much bigger than that. He cares more about what's being formed in you than what's happening around you.

Accomplishing God's purpose can only happen HIS way, and accomplishment doesn't happen in the absence of adversity, it happens because of it.

ALLOWING ADVERSITY

I don't believe that God causes bad things to happen to you (don't forget we have an enemy, the devil, whose only goal is to destroy us[3]) but I do believe that God can use those things to accomplish his purposes. The Bible refers to God as a good Father who wants to give us good things.[4] No father would be considered good if he wished harm upon his children. As a father myself, I could never imagine wanting bad things to happen to my kids.

However, really good parents lead their children into growth. They are responsible to not simply be friends with their kids but to teach them and train them, to help them grow up to become men and women of God. If parents don't teach their kids how to deal with the difficult stuff in life, they'll never be able to experience the really good stuff.

God is a really good parent! He's always going to do what's best for us, even if it's not what we think we want. Hebrews 12:5-10 phrases it like this:

> *Don't make light of the LORD's discipline, and don't give up when he corrects you. For the Lord disciplines those he loves... For our earthly fathers disciplined us for a few years, doing the best they knew how. But God's discipline is always good for us, so that we might share in his holiness.*

God is in the business of helping us grow! As he challenges us, we can actually be encouraged. It serves as proof that he loves us as his children and sees potential us.

When speaking about adversity, British speaker and author, Graham Cooke, dropped a one-liner that has become one of my favorites:

"GOD ALLOWS IN HIS WISDOM WHAT HE COULD EASILY PREVENT BY HIS POWER."

Jesus could have easily prevented the adversity Bartimaeus faced. He could easily prevent whatever you are facing right now. However, in his wisdom, he's allowing it. Your adversity is not too big for him to handle. He's not abandoning you. Rather, he is developing something in you.

Bartimaeus developed a stronger faith as he refused to be silenced in his pursuit of Jesus. As resistance increased, so did his intensity, and every shout deepened his belief that Jesus would respond. His miracle was being developed in the face of adversity.

I don't know what difficulty you may be facing, but I do know that God can use it to develop something special on the inside of you. The devil will attack you and bring adversity to your weakest areas. In his grace, God will use that adversity to strengthen you in those same areas. Therefore, every time you face adversity, it's an opportunity for exponential growth.

If you're facing financial difficulty, God can develop your trust in him as your provider. He can teach you to become generous even with very little. He can use your situation to create urgency in you to learn good stewardship.

If you find yourself consumed by anxiety or fear, God can show you how to give everything to him and experience his perfect peace and love. He wants to lead you into the freedom that he gives to his children.

If you're battling sickness, God can develop your dependency on him and show you that he is a healer. He may want to reveal his power to you in a whole new way. Your sickness could end up being the very thing that shatters areas of unbelief in your heart.

Maybe you're just tired. Going to school, working, raising kids, and all the responsibilities and pressures of life have worn you down. God wants to show you how to find your strength and restoration in him. He can teach you how to rest in the middle of chaos.

God allows adversity out of his affection for you. Some of us need to stop running from adversity and start running to God in the middle of it. We will never become the people that God has called us to be, never accomplish the things he has planned for us, without it. It's not fun to face adversity, but it's unavoidable, so we'd better develop the proper response.

RESPONDING TO ADVERSITY

Leadership expert Sam Chand says, "You will grow at the level of pain that you are willing to endure." There will be painful moments in pursuing God, but there's always growth on the other side if we're willing to stick it out. Our response to adversity plays a big part in our ability to push through the pain and experience God's blessing on the other side.

The Bible offers a unique perspective on how to respond to adversity. James 1:2-4 says:

Dear brothers and sisters, when troubles of any kind come your way, consider it an opportunity for great joy. For you know that when your faith is tested, your endurance has a chance to grow. So let it grow, for when your endurance is fully developed, you will be perfect and complete, needing nothing.

When, not if, we face trouble, instead of getting upset about it, we have the opportunity to be joyful. To be honest, it's hard for me to be joyful about hardship. That's not the way that our human minds are naturally wired! We want to have easy, comfortable lives, so when adversity threatens our comfort and security, we tend to get angry, run from it, or both. However, God's Word gives us an invitation to stand firm and stay the course.

When we welcome challenges, we form faith to trust God to get us through, not just this time, but the next time, and the next. When we don't let the difficulties derail us, we learn to persevere toward the promise.

Adversity might be the last place you expect to find God, but if you open your eyes, he's always there. That's why we can have joy in the middle of struggles, because it's through these tests that we develop the character and strength that God wants us to have.

Like gold being refined by fire, like diamonds forming under intense pressure, adversity, like it or not, is what makes us more like Jesus.

Jesus faced more adversity than we ever will (not only was he tortured and crucified – he took all the sin of all humanity on himself, so, yeah, I'd say that's a lot) yet had joy through it because he knew he was doing it for *you*. Hebrews 12:2-3 explains:

> *Because of the joy awaiting him, [Jesus] endured the cross, disregarding its shame. Now he is seated in the place of honor beside God's throne. Think of all the hostility he endured from sinful people; then you won't become weary and give up.*

Learning to rejoice in suffering seems to go against our nature, but it's responding to adversity with joy that will actually get you through it!

HOW WELL CAN YOU SEE?

I've found that there's one key thing that separates people who can handle adversity and those who can't: vision. People who have a strong vision for where they want to go are often able to withstand strong adversity to get there.

The vision to defeat Mike Tyson would have to be big enough to withstand some knockout punches. My vision for our church is bigger than the obstacles that we have faced. Bartimaeus' vision to see again (that's not a joke) was bigger than the will of the people who tried to silence him.

YOUR VISION FOR WHERE YOU'RE GOING MUST BE GREATER THAN ANY ADVERSITY YOU WILL FACE.

That doesn't mean the adversity that comes your way won't seem really big. In fact, I know that it will be! What this means is that you better get a vision that's really, really big! Your vision has to be God-sized.

My definition of vision is the ability to think about, plan for, or see the future. It's the ability to see past where you are and imagine where you can go. People with vision can see how their marriages, finances, personal lives, careers, or businesses would look if they made some improvements and innovations. They don't accept the status quo, they push for progress.

A God-sized vision takes into account that God wants to be involved. Ephesians 3:20 says that God is able, "through his mighty power at work within us, to accomplish infinitely more than we might ask or think."

God-sized vision is bigger than man-sized vision. Our vision is rooted in what we can do, but God's vision is all about what HE can do. If vision is about our ability to think, then we have to realize that God can accomplish "infinitely more than we might ask or think!"

If our vision needs to be greater than the adversity we face, then it has to come from God. God's vision for your life is the only vision that is worth pursuing anyway.

It's better than anything that you could imagine for yourself.

Without a vision from God for your life, you will wander around aimlessly, and adversity will constantly throw you off course. Proverbs 29:18 (TPT) says,

> *When there is no clear prophetic vision, people quickly wander astray. But when you follow the revelation of the word, heaven's bliss fills your soul.*

Other translations say that without vision people "perish."[5] They may not experience physical death, but their dreams, relationships, or moral compasses will be destroyed. When you lose the vision, you lose the fight. If you aren't able to stand firm on *why* you're doing what you're doing, adversity will convince you that it's not worth it anymore.

How do we develop a God-sized vision? How can we make sure that our vision is strong enough to push through adversity?

Proverbs 29:18 goes on to explain that when we receive revelation from the Word, then our souls are filled with Heaven's bliss! What the heck does that mean? Let me attempt an explanation.

Revelation is when God supernaturally reveals something to us with the intent of empowering us in our pursuit of him and his purpose. The Bible (God's written word) is one of the primary tools that God uses to help us learn more about him. The more that we dive into the Bible, the more we begin to discover who God is and how to distinguish his voice from others in our lives. He starts to help us comprehend things like how much he loves us and how big his purpose is for us. He begins to show us what he values – things like purity, holiness, and the way that we love.

Vision is related to the revelation that we get from the Bible. As we get a deeper understanding of God through his Word, we will more easily identify his vision for our lives. Here's why:

ANY VISION THAT GOD HAS FOR MY LIFE WILL LINE UP WITH WHAT HE VALUES.

For example, God's vision for you will revolve around loving him, loving others, and putting them before yourself.[6] It won't oppose his mission or contradict his standards. He will use the unique spiritual gifts that he has given you to help others and ultimately to bring him glory.[7]

When you get to know the truest things about God and who he is, you will be able to discern when he is speaking something to you about your future. It will line up with what he values. And when you are confident that God gave you vision, you can hold on to that vision in the face of adversity.

Vision motivates us to take risks. It inspires us to reach for new heights. At times, it might even lead us to be a little bit reckless. It gives us the confidence to go after things that we could never accomplish in our own strength. When you experience the revelation of how big God is, how vast his love, how great his plans, that vision can lead you into the unknown with courage and determination.

———

Bartimaeus may not have had sight, but he had vision. He knew that on his own, he could do nothing to be able to see again or to get out of the wayside. But he also knew who Jesus was.

Bartimaeus knew that the Savior, the Son of David, the King of Kings could do the impossible in his life. His God-sized vision wasn't just about healing his blindness, it was about redeeming his entire life. This God-sized vision was greater than the adversity he faced.

What adversity are you facing? Do you have a vision that is bigger? If not, you are missing out. God has amazing plans for your life. Even though you may not know all of the details yet, he wants to get you on the right path, headed in the direction of the purpose that he has for you.

I want to encourage you to pray for joy to overcome adversity, but also pray that God would give you vision. Allow him to develop character in you so that you can become the person he needs you to be and to go to the places he's called you to go!

FIVE

REFLECTION + APPLICATION

Do you run from adversity? Ask God to help you see adversity as something helpful rather than hurtful.

_____

_____

_____

What might God be trying to develop in you through the current adversity you are facing?

_____

_____

_____

Do you have a vision for your life? Ask God to reveal to you where he wants to take you.

_____

_____

_____

How often do you read the Bible? Make a goal that includes a constant reading plan. The more that you dive in, the more you can understand who God is and what he has for you.

_____

_____

_____

CHAPTER SIX

STOPPING JESUS

**WHEN JESUS
HEARD HIM,
HE STOPPED
AND SAID,
"TELL HIM TO
COME HERE."**

MARK 10:49

Have you been ignored by those around you? Have you ever felt forgotten?

Bartimaeus was used to being ignored. He lived in the reality of being neglected and forgotten. You already know that because of his blindness, Bartimaeus had no way to make a living. He couldn't work in the fields, learn a trade, or sell goods at the marketplace. Bartimaeus had to beg to survive.

In almost every city I travel to, I see beggars. Even on opposite sides of the country, there is one common denominator I observe: beggars are often ignored. They're fully dependent on the generosity of those who pass by, but the people passing are usually too busy, too hurried, too preoccupied, or too indifferent to stop in their tracks.

I can imagine that after being passed by time and

time again, you start to feel discouraged. Discouragement can quickly affect how you think of yourself. You start to wonder if you are unimportant. You come to believe that you are unlovable, unworthy.

This is the reality of Bartimaeus' life. For years, he was overlooked. Rejection was normal. Neglect was his daily bread. Yet Bartimaeus continued to beg because it was his only hope to eat that day. It was his only shot at survival. And every day, hundreds of people would pass the beggar sitting in the sewer without thinking twice. They never put themselves in his shoes (he probably didn't have any shoes) or tried to understand what it was like to be blind or unable to work. They probably had the means to help, but had too little compassion or too much disgust.

But on *this* day, even though Bartimaeus was ignored by men, he was noticed by Jesus. As Jesus heard Bartimaeus shouting to him, he stopped dead in his tracks. Bartimaeus had called out to others before, and they had passed him by. But when this blind beggar cried out for mercy in the middle of his mess, the God of the universe stopped and responded!

You may feel like you've been passed over in life. It might seem like nobody recognizes your value. You may think you've been forgotten. But if Jesus didn't forget Bartimaeus, then he hasn't forgotten about you!

JESUS NOTICES THOSE THAT OTHERS NEGLECT.

Bartimaeus could do nothing for Jesus. He had nothing to offer – no money, no influence, no resources. Bartimaeus sat in stark contrast to the crowds of people that were swarming around Jesus. Remember, Jericho was a wealthy city. Many of the people had access to resources and power. They had wealth that they could offer to Jesus. They had influence that they could have leveraged for him.

Yet Jesus didn't stop for them; he stopped for the poorest, most broken, most desperate beggar. He stopped for the one who had been passed over. He stopped for the one who was neglected. He stopped for the one who was cast aside. He noticed and he stopped.

In the same way that Jesus noticed Bartimaeus, I can promise, he notices you.

A SEAT AT THE TABLE

I've been lucky enough to become friends with some amazing pastors across the country. I often get invited to their conferences and workshops that are tailored for church leadership, strategy, and growth. When Rust City was about four years old, I was invited to a church "Round Table" event. The purpose of the event was to collaborate with others who were in the same area of ministry as you to sharpen one another, generate new ideas, and grow as a leader.

The event was about four hours away, but I really loved the pastor who invited me, so I decided to go and also to bring our entire staff and ministry school with me. There would be specific training for each area of ministry, so I was excited about giving my team a chance to broaden their perspective, learn from leaders in their field, and be inspired to grow.

It was a big commitment to bring our entire team of thirty people and pay the way for all of them! We covered gas, hotel stay, and food. The trip ended up costing us thousands of dollars. As a young church, or really as a church in any season, dropping that much money on one event can be stressful. However, I was confident that the investment would be worth it.

When we arrived at the Round Table, we realized that we had brought more people than any other church. There were about ninety people in attendance, and thirty of them were from Rust City Church! That means one in every three people was there with me. We felt honored to have such a presence at an event like this. Our staff and students were dispersed at tables all across the room – our campus pastors at the campus pastor table, the youth team at the youth table, kids team at the kids table, admin team at the admin table. There was one table reserved for senior pastors. They got to hang out, collaborate, and learn from the host of the event. As I made my way over to that table, I quickly realized that there was no seat for me.

Looking around, hoping no one noticed the awkwardness I felt, I discovered that my reserved spot was at the campus pastors' table. As I took my seat among the campus pastors who worked for me, and campus pastors from other churches, I was hurt. I love campus pastors, but I wasn't a campus pastor!

To make matters worse, some of the dialogue at this table revolved around the tension that can exist while working for your senior pastor. For example, the first question discussed was, "How do you respond when your senior pastor asks you to do something that you don't want to do?" While all of the other campus pastors were speaking freely, my campus pastors were hesitant to open up about how they felt and gave super generic answers with awkward side glances at me – their boss – sitting right next to them. As uncomfortable as they felt, I can guarantee you, I felt way worse!

I couldn't help continually gazing across the room at the table of senior pastors. The more I looked, the more frustrated I got. I brought more people, generated more income for the event, and drove further than any other church to be there, yet I had still been overlooked. Throughout the day, for eight long hours, it continued to eat away at me.

As the event was coming to an end, my frustration had boiled to the point that I was ready to get up and tell the host pastor that what he did to me was wrong. The speech I had prepared in my mind over the last several hours eloquently expressed the injustice committed against me, and, in all honesty, probably would have burned bridges and ruined our friendship. Right before I got up from my chair, I whispered a prayer to God. "Help me, Lord. What do you want me to do right now?"

As clear as day, I could sense God whispering back to me, "Doug, even though you feel forgotten by your peers, I will never forget you. It doesn't matter what they think of you; what matters is how I think about you. You didn't have a seat at their table but you will always have a seat at mine."

Before God spoke to me, I felt like Bartimaeus sitting by the wayside. I was trying so hard to build a church and do it well. I was doing everything I knew how to do to train my team and expand the church, but it still wasn't enough to be noticed or recognized among other pastors. I was neglected and overlooked. But as soon as Jesus reminded me that I would always have a seat at his table, all of the frustration inside of me dissipated. I experienced an overwhelming peace and sense of belonging.

WHEN YOU REALIZE JESUS REMEMBERS YOU, IT DOESN'T MATTER WHO HAS FORGOTTEN YOU.

How do you feel as you're reading this? Do you feel forgotten? Maybe you're a single mother whose efforts have gone unnoticed. You could be a father working extra hours to provide for your family, yet you feel underappreciated. Maybe you've been serving at church and nobody ever says thank you. Perhaps you've been diligently trying to share the love of Jesus with those around you and they don't seem to care. Maybe you've been working hard as a pastor for a really long time, and it doesn't seem like your church or community is responding to you. Even if you feel forgotten, God has not forgotten about you!

———

As human beings, we naturally crave affirmation. It feels good to be loved and appreciated by those around you. We want to be recognized by our spouse, kids, coworkers, boss, classmates, friends – anybody, really. It's not wrong to desire approval. God uniquely designed us to be able to love and be loved. However, where we seek our validation matters.

In a letter to the church in Ephesus, the apostle Paul encourages believers about this very thing:

> *May you have the power to understand, as all God's people should, how wide, how long, how high, and how deep his love is. May you experience the love of Christ, though it is too great to understand fully. Then you will be made complete with all the fullness of life and power that comes from God.[1]*

Paul does an amazing job of expressing how incredible God's love is. Even after explaining the vastness of God's love, he still says that we can never understand it fully. However, the Scripture explains that the more we experience the love of Christ and grasp what it means for us, the more we will be made complete.

Maybe you've been looking for a person to say "you complete me" or trying to fill the void in your life in any way possible. The truth is, you'll only feel complete when

EVEN IF YOU FEEL FORGOTTEN GOD HAS NOT FORGOTTEN ABOUT YOU

you start to see yourself through the love God has for you.

God's love, not anything else, is what leads to our wholeness. It is the driving force that empowers us to live! Our primary source of affirmation and affection should be our Heavenly Father, not the people around us. Knowing God loves us gives us security, confidence, and hope, even when everything else says otherwise.

For those of you reading this who feel like you haven't received the affirmation you deserve from those around you, you may be right. But as long as you're looking for affirmation from other human beings, you will continue to be disappointed and unsatisfied. More than likely, people are not intentionally withholding approval from you, rather, they are busy seeking it themselves. They can't give you what they don't have.

My prayer for you is that you would stop seeking affirmation from others and start understanding God's affection for you. When you recognize how immense his affection is, your need for affirmation will grow smaller.

WE CARE A LOT ABOUT RECOGNITION FROM OTHERS WHEN WE FAIL TO RECOGNIZE GOD'S AFFECTION FOR US.

Recognizing the affection that God has for you will change the way that you approach him. When you truly start to understand how crazy he is about you, it will change the way that you call out to him. As you develop confidence in the fact that you are his beloved child, you will naturally become more aggressive in your pursuit of his miracles in your life.

The Bible says in Ephesians 4:2-6 (NIV) that "because of his great love for us, God, who is rich in mercy... raised us up with Christ and *seated us with him.*" Even when you don't get awarded on earth, your reward still awaits you in Heaven. Even when others don't notice you, God does. You have a seat at his table.

THE SHOUT THAT STOPPED JESUS

When Jesus passed through Jericho in Mark 10, he was headed into the most significant season of his life. Right before Jesus came into contact with Bartimaeus, he explained to his disciples what was about to happen at the end of their journey:

> *They were now on the way up to Jerusalem, and Jesus was walking ahead of them. The disciples were filled with awe, and the people following behind were overwhelmed with fear. Taking the twelve disciples aside, Jesus once more began to describe everything that was about to happen to him. "Listen," he said, "we're going up to Jerusalem, where the Son of Man will be betrayed to the leading priests and the teachers of religious law. They will sentence him to die and hand him over to the Romans. They will mock him, spit on him, flog him with a whip, and kill him, but after three days he will rise again."[2]*

Jesus wasn't on just another trip, he was on his last trip! When he arrived in Jerusalem, it wouldn't just be another opportunity for him to do ministry, it would be time for him to fulfill his destiny. The primary reason that Jesus came to Earth was to die on the cross and rise from the grave. In doing so, he'd make a way for people like you and me to receive eternal life, freedom from sin, and a renewed relationship with God. Still, Jesus knew that leaving Jericho that day meant walking the final road to death.

Looking at it from that perspective, it would be pretty excusable if Jesus didn't stop for Bartimaeus. I picture this as a scene from one of my favorite action movies. Jesus is ready for battle. The musical score is intensifying as he steps out (in slow motion) on the road. Dust rises as he takes each step. His entourage can be seen walking in ranks behind Jesus. A close up of his eyes, fierce with the fire of determination, as he mentally prepares to take out the enemy. His pace quickens. He shouts, "Bring me Thanos!" – wait, wrong movie!

Seriously, though, Jesus was literally about to defeat the power of sin and death. I think that would require some intense focus.

On top of that, Jesus had to be experiencing some unsettled emotion. He is fully God, but also fully man, which means he felt the same hurt, pain, and fear that we feel. He knew that when he arrived in Jerusalem, the very people he came to save would falsely accuse him of crimes he didn't commit. He knew that one of his closest friends would betray him. He would be mocked, spat upon, flogged with a lead-tipped whip, and beaten beyond the point of recognition. He would go to the cross, become the sin of humanity, be separated from God, and die the most burdensome, painful death in history.

I don't know how to adequately suppose what that would feel like. I can't imagine the type of stress it would produce. The Bible says that right before his arrest, while praying in the Garden of Gethsemane, Jesus was sweating out drops of blood! The physical, mental, and spiritual toll of what was about to happen to him was so heavy that he was sweating blood. Can you imagine that kind of pressure?

I know that Jesus came to serve others, but I could understand in this moment if he needed some "me" time. I wouldn't have been surprised if Jesus was so laser-focused on his mission that he never even heard Bartimaeus.

Bartimaeus probably wasn't aware of what Jesus was on his way to do. He didn't know Jesus was on his way to save the entire world, but he knew that Jesus could save him. So he shouted and shouted, believing wholeheartedly that God's mercy would even extend to one blind beggar.

When Bartimaeus shouted, Jesus stopped. Even though he was busy, focused, stressed, and walking to his death, he stopped! Why?

Again, it's not because Bartimaeus had it all together or had anything to offer. Matthew's account of this story says Jesus was "deeply moved with compassion."[3]

When Bartimaeus shouted, it activated the compassion of Jesus. When Bartimaeus shouted, it was as a child of God who desperately needed help. When Bartimaeus shouted, it was with faith that Jesus could do the impossible in his life. When Bartimaeus shouted, Jesus stopped. And in the same way that Bartimaeus had Jesus' ear, you can have it as well.

YOUR CALL ACTIVATES THE COMPASSION OF JESUS. YOUR SHOUT STOPS HIM DEAD IN HIS TRACKS!

One of the incredible things about Jesus is that even though he never sinned, he understands what it's like to be tested and tempted. He understands what we are going through and empathizes with us. Because of that, the Bible says that we have permission to approach God boldly. Hebrews 4:15-16 says:

> *This High Priest of ours understands our weaknesses, for he faced all of the same testings we do, yet he did not sin. So let us come boldly to the throne of our gracious God. There we will receive his mercy, and we will find grace to help us when we need it most.*

We're invited to come to receive mercy and grace. Jesus meets us, not with condemnation, but with compassion. It's the type of compassion that forgives us, but also frees us to live out God's best for our lives.

Because of Jesus, you have one-hundred-percent, full

access to God. He'll stop for your shout. His compassion has drawn him toward you and he is waiting for you to call out. He wants to get all up-close-and-personal with you. He sees you. He hears you. He loves you. He can help you. Maybe the only thing standing between you and the fullness of his power in your life is your shout.

THE HUNGER OF A CHILD

Jesus' response to Bartimaeus' shout reminds me of when my sister, Katie, had her first child, Ava.

Katie was an amazing first-time mother, but maybe also a little bit of a psycho first-time mother. When I say psycho, I'm referring to the fact that she was more prepared for how to raise a child than any mother in the history of humanity. She had read every parenting book. She subscribed to every blog about motherhood. She knew every strategy for raising the perfect child.

One of the things that Katie really focused on was Ava's feeding schedule. In attempts to maximize Ava's nap times and energy cycles (pretty intense stuff for a little baby), Katie fed her at the exact same times every single day, precisely as her favorite blog post had told her. She believed that this would lead her child to become an Olympian, doctor, or something crazy along those lines.

Kudos to Katie. However, if you've ever been a parent before, you know that children are unpredictable. Just like the boxers we talked about in the last chapter, every parent has a plan until they get punched in the face! More often than not, the plan gets tossed out of the window.

A couple of weeks into having Ava at home, Katie's plan was put to the test. In the middle of the night, Ava started crying. She wasn't just shedding a few tears; this was top of her lungs, gasping for breath, ear-piercing wailing! Nothing that Katie tried to comfort her baby would work. She soon realized that Ava only wanted one thing – milk!

Katie had a decision to make. Do I follow the plan or do I feed my daughter? At that moment, her motherly instinct kicked in. Even though it went against everything she had read, learned, and planned, she fed Ava.

Why? Because good parents respond to the hunger of their children.

GOD IS A GOOD FATHER, AND HE RESPONDS TO THE HUNGER OF HIS CHILDREN!

Ava expressed her hunger the only way she knew how, to the only person she knew could help her. She didn't care that the timing was inconvenient. She didn't consider whether Katie had other things to do. She cried out in need and trusted her parent to respond.

When Bartimaeus cried out, the timing wasn't convenient for Jesus, who was on his way to take care of bigger things, but he still responded. And when you cry out in hunger, God will respond to you.

I love how Jesus responded after he heard Bartimaeus and stopped: "Tell him to come here."

Tell him to come to me.

COME TO ME.

God's response to your cries will always contain an invitation. God doesn't just want to meet your need, he wants to invite you to more.

God is relationally motivated. He does not live in a galaxy far, far away. When you accept Jesus into your life, his own Spirit comes to live inside you. He wants to be involved in your daily life and unleash his power in every situation. He wants a relationship.

James 4:8 says,

Come close to God and God will come close to you.

When you take steps toward God, he takes steps back toward you. His invitation to come to him means, as a child of God, you are always welcome. He wants you to come to him with every need; he'll never turn you away. But I believe it's also an invitation to see how hungry you really are.

How hungry are you for God? Do you just want him to take care of your problems, or do you want a real relationship with him? Do you pray just to check off a box, or do you pray because you genuinely desire to see his will unfold in your life? Do you have a hunger to learn more about God from his Word, or are you distracted and consumed by other things? Are you desperate to live in freedom from sin, or are the desires of your flesh greater than your desire for the Holy Spirit?

I want to encourage you to live in such a way that you are constantly developing a deeper hunger for God. The same desire that children have for their earthly parents is the same desire that your Heavenly Father wants from you. And when he sees it, he is drawn to it.

In my pursuit of God, I've found that if you always do what you've always done, you'll always get what you've always got. If you want something different, you have to do some things differently. God is not stagnant. He's unchanging, but he's also infinite, so there will always be more for you to discover about him. The dynamics of your relationship will forever be shifting. To have new experiences with him, we have to stretch our pursuit outside of our comfort zone.

For example, maybe instead of praying in your head, try praying out loud. Instead of praying in the same tone of voice that you use in everyday conversation, try taking your passion up a level.

If you typically only sing during worship, try lifting your hands. If you've become comfortable lifting your hands, try getting on your knees. Let the desperation for Jesus on the inside of you authentically flow out of you.

Instead of just reading the Bible for information, start claiming the promises of the Word over your life. Repeat them out loud and believe them.

If you've become comfortable serving people within the confines of your church, try serving someone outside of those four walls. Demonstrate the love of Jesus to someone in public. Invite them to church. Be willing to step outside of your comfort zone.

God responds to hunger, and he is ready to respond to yours.

———

Bartimaeus' life was forever changed by Jesus because he believed that God had not forgotten about him. In the middle of his mess, he cried out for mercy. Moved with compassion, Jesus not only noticed his hunger, but honored his hunger and invited him to come closer to a miracle.

Before you finish this chapter, take a moment and ask Jesus to stop what he's doing and be with you. Give him full access to your life and everything going on in it. Pray that he would increase your hunger for him.

God has not forgotten about you. He is inviting you to come to him. He is ready and willing to get involved in your mess and show you mercy.

SIX

REFLECTION + APPLICATION

Do you feel forgotten by those around you? Ask God to heal those areas of your heart.

_____

_____

_____

Do you believe that God's affection is enough for you? Pray that his love would fill the empty areas of your life.

_____

_____

_____

Do you have a vision for your life? Ask God to reveal to you where he wants to take you.

_____

_____

_____

How hungry are you for God? What can you do to step out of your comfort zone in your pursuit of him?

_____

_____

_____

CHAPTER SEVEN

THE DEVIL'S TRAP

**SO THEY CALLED
THE BLIND MAN.
"CHEER UP,"
THEY SAID.
"COME ON, HE'S
CALLING YOU!"**

MARK 10:49

Before we dive into this chapter, let's do a quick refresher. In Chapter 4, we talked about haters – the crowds of people who surrounded Jesus and tried to prevent Bartimaeus from calling out and receiving his miracle.

In case you forgot, in Mark 10:48, which was just one short verse ago, these people told Bartimaeus to shut his mouth when he was shouting. They didn't think that a blind beggar was worthy of Jesus' attention, or that Jesus would ever stop, so they tried to silence a nuisance.

Isn't it interesting that, moments later, the same people who told Bartimaeus to *be quiet* are now telling him to *cheer up*? The same people who told him to stop are now the ones telling him to go. They tried to prevent his miracle and now they're encouraging him to come and get it!

They hopped on what I like to call the "Bartimaeus Bandwagon."

When my Cleveland Browns signed Odell Beckham, Jr. in free agency, "fans" came out of nowhere to cheer for them. Those same fans weren't around two years prior, agonizing with me when the Browns went 0-16. But when they anticipated something special might happen, they wanted to be a part of it.

In the same way, once Jesus acknowledged Bartimaeus, the crowds who snubbed him became his biggest fans. People who walked past Bartimaeus every day as he begged, and never acknowledged or supported him, suddenly acted like his BFFs!

They weren't coming from a place of genuine care for Bartimaeus. Rather, they figured if Jesus was going to do something special in Bartimaeus' life, then maybe they could benefit, too. They weren't interested in a genuine relationship with Bartimaeus, they just wanted to attach themselves to his miracle.

Be aware of people who didn't want anything to do with you before God touched your life, but want something from you now that he has. When God does something special inside of you, he will bring people into your life for you to minister to – that's what God has called us to do. However, be cautious of the ones who seem as if they want to be on your inner circle only for what they can get out of you.

Your closest relationships should be built on the foundation of God growing your lives together. You should uplift, encourage, support, love, and challenge one another in all seasons. There is give and take in every relationship, but your closest friendships should have more balance, and be mutually beneficial. You should be able to run every relationship through that filter to determine how deep of a relationship it should be.

I'm not suggesting that you be mean or judgmental towards people who only want to jump on board when you've got a good thing going, but I am saying that there's a limit to how much access to your life they should have. The amount of influence bandwagoners have on you should be minimal. If they suddenly want to support you and what you're doing – great! But you should never alter your course just to keep people on your wagon. How you serve God and make decisions should be to please God, not to keep people happy. If others like it, that's great, but if they don't, that's okay as well.

It's interesting to me how Bartimaeus responded to his bandwagon fans. When they were his haters, he ignored them as they tried to stop his shouting. After they became his fans and encouraged him, he still ignored them. He never acknowledged them in either scenario.

Bartimaeus' pursuit of Jesus was never about the crowd. So if they wanted to hate him for the way he pursued Jesus, fine! And if they wanted to support him for the way he pursued Jesus, fine! They were not his motivation. They were not his influence. They were not who he was trying to impress. So regardless of what the crowds did, Bartimaeus kept doing Bartimaeus.

His pursuit of Jesus was the same whether anybody paid attention to him or not. He didn't change because he was suddenly popular.

The enemy would have loved to use Bartimaeus' newfound popularity. If Bartimaeus would have started focusing on his popularity instead of his purpose, if he would have paid more attention to the people who finally noticed him than he did to his pursuit of Jesus, then he might have missed out on his miracle.

THE DEVIL CAN USE POPULARITY TO DISTRACT YOU FROM YOUR PURPOSE.

When God starts to move in your life, there is a temptation to become preoccupied with the popularity it may initially bring you. It's easy to become fixated on things like affirmation from others, compliments, and the number of followers or likes we get on social media.

If I'm being honest, there's a temptation to "humblebrag" when God starts to use you. A humblebrag is when you boast about your success but then pretend not to take credit for it by saying "God is good" or "I'm blessed." Even pastors can struggle with this. Whenever I go to pastors' conferences or gatherings, it's easy for us pastors to talk about how many people attend our church, how many campuses we have, and if we aren't careful, we can make it all about numbers. Conversations can quickly turn into competitions.

Don't get me wrong, God is doing something special at all of our churches. He is doing things that should be celebrated! However, significance isn't defined by a specific number or threshold of success. It's easy to fall into the trap of talking about what God has done through us to make ourselves feel good, rather than to simply celebrate his goodness. The reality is, none of us got into ministry because it would make us popular; we did it because we felt a sense of purpose. However, just as he tried with Bartimaeus, the devil will try to entice you with chasing popularity rather than chasing purpose.

I want to encourage you, don't let the distraction of popularity deter you from your God-given purpose. Your pursuit of Jesus is not contingent on the approval of others. Your followers on Instagram are not more important than the investment that you make into people. The impressiveness of your success will not sustain you. Only Jesus and the purpose he has for you can do that.

Bartimaeus never acknowledged his sudden popularity. He didn't say, "Finally, the influential and wealthy people of Jericho have noticed me! This is the moment I've been waiting for!" He kept his focus on Jesus. He stayed fixated on his miracle. He continued to chase after God's purpose. Every day, you have the ability to make the same choice.

POPULARITY VS PURPOSE

I'm a firm believer that we should regularly take inventory of the condition of our hearts. David said in Psalm 139:23, "Search me, O God, and know my heart..."

Most people who serve God have good intentions,

but we serve God in a world that is influenced by sin. We are constantly under the attack of the enemy. If we aren't careful, our intentions can be influenced. We can become motivated by things of this world without even noticing.

The Bible says that "no one can serve two masters."[1] We may be attempting to serve God, but sometimes end up serving our own selfish purposes without even realizing it. That's why it's so important to consistently check what is motivating us. It's crucial to evaluate what is really driving us.

There are obvious differences between people driven by popularity and people driven by purpose. As we take a few minutes to dive into what those differences are, I want to challenge you to search your heart. Ask God to point out anything in you that wasn't placed there by him. If you feel convicted about the condition of your heart, it's not because God is upset with you. It's his love for you attempting to get you back in alignment with his heart and the perfect purpose he has for you.

1. POPULARITY SEEKS THE APPROVAL OF PEERS, PURPOSE SEEKS THE APPROVAL OF GOD.

If you're a person driven by popularity, you will constantly be worrying about what other people think about you. You'll be consumed by what your boss thought of your presentation, whether your mother approved of your decision, if your kids are mad at you because you punished them, or what your friends think of your new relationship.

Don't get me wrong, wisdom can be found in other people's advice. As we talked about earlier, you should receive wisdom from those who you want to be like. However, God doesn't want you to be consumed with everyone else's opinion of you.

God invites us to seek him, to live according to his standard, and to make decisions based on his direction. Sometimes, those decisions are tough. Furthermore, those decisions are often unpopular.

In John 15:19, Jesus gives a warning:

"If you belonged to the world, it would love you as its own. As it is, you do not belong to the world, but I have chosen you out of the world. That is why the world hates you."

Jesus is letting us know that what will earn the approval of the world is not necessarily what he approves. What he loves may be what the world hates. He's reminding us that his purpose for us is more important than our popularity. We can find freedom from needing approval from everyone all the time, because the only true approval that we need comes from God.

2. POPULARITY REQUIRES FOLLOWERS, PURPOSE REQUIRES FRUITFULNESS.

We tend to equate success with size. If a lot of people are a part of it, or it looks big, or has over 10,000 followers, it must be good. While I do believe that healthy things grow, it's not only the biggest things that can be fruitful.

In Matthew 25, Jesus teaches what is referred to as the "Parable of the Talents." He compares our lives to servants who are entrusted with resources when their master goes on a trip. The master gives his servants either one, two, or five "talents" (large sums of money). Those who do well with what they are given are entrusted with more. Those who do nothing with what they are given have it taken away.

The obvious lesson is that if God can trust us with what he gives, he will give us even more responsibility and opportunity, but if he cannot trust us, he won't. However, what has always stuck out to me is that each of the servants were initially entrusted with different amounts. Some less and some more.

God is not so much concerned with the size of what we are doing, but rather that we are taking good care of what we have been given. It's easy to think that God is only in something if we have a large following, however, God is more concerned with faithfulness and fruitfulness. He wants to see that what we have been given, whether large or small, is being taken care of and is growing, regardless what that scale of growth is.

If we aren't careful, we can neglect God-given opportunities because we don't think they will produce a lot of followers. God doesn't care about your following, he cares about your fruit.

Fruit is produced by staying connected to God and being a good steward of what he gives you. God wants to free you from the pressure of gaining followers, and invite you into the meaningfulness of producing fruit.

3. POPULARITY NEEDS CONSTANT AFFIRMATION, PURPOSE NEEDS CONSTANT EFFECTIVENESS.

As we talked about in the last chapter, we all enjoy hearing "great job" from other people. While it's helpful to be encouraged by others, there will be times in your journey that you might have to push towards purpose without encouragement from anybody besides God himself.

Purpose is more concerned with effectiveness than affirmation. To be effective is to produce results. There are results that God wants to produce through you that might not stir up compliments and affirmation from other people. In fact, they might be met with opposition.

For example, the decision to discipline your children might not be met with an affirming response from them. My kids have never said, "Thanks, Dad, I appreciate you sending me to my room. I know that being a father is full of making tough decisions, and I'm so thankful that you have the wisdom to be able to do the things that are best for me!" Most of the time they cry, scream, and let me know that they hate me! However, Proverbs 3:12 (NIV) says that "the Lord disciplines those he loves." It's my responsibility to father my children the way that God fathers me. Just because they don't affirm all of my decisions doesn't mean that they aren't the right decisions. God calls us to be effective, even in the absence of affirmation.

4. POPULARITY SEEKS COMFORT,
PURPOSE SEEKS GROWTH.

Much of our desire for popularity is produced from our desire to be comfortable. We create false ideas in our mind that if everyone likes us or we achieve some level of status, that we will finally be comfortable and find the fulfillment we've desired.

The irony is that along with popularity comes scrutiny. Popularity gives more people a window into your life. The more people who can see what is going on in your world, the more criticism comes your way. Popularity doesn't bring comfort, it brings the opposite.

Purpose understands that growth comes at the cost of comfort. Haven't you heard of growing pains? Whenever God wants to do something in or through us, it always challenges our comfort.

As Jesus is describing his own ministry, he makes a polarizing statement about the nature of it:

> *"Foxes have dens to live in, and birds have nests,*
> *but the Son of Man has no place even to lay his*
> *head."*

Most of us reading this have a home we go to every night. It's where you can let your guard down, relax, and feel at peace. Home is a representation of comfort. When Jesus said he had no place to lay his head, he's showing us that he lived his life in a way that wasn't comfortable! He had the love, grace, and peace of the Father on his side, but as he pursued his purpose, his own comfort took a back seat.

In the same way, if you want to fulfill God's purpose for your life, you have to drop the facade that popularity will bring the security you desire. You must accept the fact that you will spend the majority of your time outside your comfort zone.

5. POPULARITY SURROUNDS YOU WITH "YES MEN," PURPOSE SURROUNDS YOU WITH HONEST FRIENDS.

If you're consumed with being popular, you will only allow people who always agree with you to speak into your life. Because you can't handle the pain of being contradicted, you will remove anyone from your life who challenges things that you say or do, even if it's out of love. That's why some of us quit jobs, leave churches, remove ourselves from relationships, and burn bridges with others.

If you are going to fulfill your God-given purpose, you need to surround yourself with people who will sharpen you. Proverbs 27:17 (NIV) says,

> As iron sharpens iron, so one person sharpens another.

The people who will sharpen you most are not necessarily those who will always agree with you. Rather, when you surround yourself with honest friends and mentors, who tell you the truth even when it hurts, they'll broaden your perspective and challenge you to be all God has called you to be. They help take you from where you currently are to where God wants you to go.

To fulfill your purpose, you have to surround yourself with the right people.

6. POPULARITY ELEVATES SELF, PURPOSE ELEVATES OTHERS.

As you serve Jesus, you will inevitably start to make an impact on the world and gain influence with those around you. If you aren't careful, you can fall into the trap of using your platform to elevate your own agenda rather than continuing to elevate and serve others.

Popularity is all about self-promotion and self-worth. It's self-centered. But if you read the Bible in any length, you will discover that God's purpose for us is to move from selfish to selfless. We were not created to seek our own glory, but to bring God the glory he deserves. Philippians 3:3-11 says:

> *Don't be selfish; don't try to impress others. Be humble, thinking of others as better than yourselves. Don't look out only for your own interests, but take an interest in others, too.*
> *You must have the same attitude that Christ Jesus had. Though he was God, he did not think of equality with God as something to cling to. Instead, he gave up his divine privileges; he took*

the humble position of a slave and was born as a
human being. When he appeared in human form,
he humbled himself in obedience to God and died
a criminal's death on a cross.

Our whole purpose is to become more like Jesus, and he gave up his life to serve and save others. This is the opposite of what the world teaches us. It's the opposite of what our selfish nature desires. But by loving God first and loving others as much as we love ourselves, we more accurately represent who Jesus actually is.

Chasing popularity will make you feel good about yourself for a little while, but chasing purpose will bring a deeper fulfillment and joy that only comes through laying down your interests and your life for others.

God's purpose for you will always benefit others. He wants you to stay humble so at the right time *he* can lift you up. The ultimate picture of Jesus elevating others over himself happened when he went to the cross. He died to save those who were his enemies, but then, Philippians goes on to say that God elevated Jesus to the place of highest honor! Laying down his life was the only way for God's purpose to advance. In the same way, the only way for God's purpose to advance through you is for you to elevate others above yourself.

PURPOSEFUL PRIORITIES

If I said the name Billy Graham, most of you would probably know who I meant. He was a pastor who left a mark not only on the church, but also in the world. His legacy echoes throughout recent history.

Born on November 7, 1918, Billy Graham grew up on a small dairy farm in North Carolina. He spent most of his time helping on his parents farm, but used his free time as an opportunity to read various books. He became hungry to experience life.

At age fifteen, God showed up and fulfilled that hunger when Billy gave his life to Jesus after hearing a traveling evangelist preach. He then decided to follow the purpose that God had given him and go into ministry.

He pastored a church before he found himself traveling around the country to preach. He became known for his crusades, and preached at his first one in Los Angeles in 1949. He would go on to speak in villages, churches, conference centers, and stadiums across the world. His influence was extensive; he spent time with presidents and leaders of many countries.[2]

Graham was not only successful, he was well-liked. Sixty-one times he finished in the Gallup's list of top ten most admired men in the world. Throughout his ministry, an estimated 2.2 billion people came to hear him preach, and approximately 2.2 million of those people came to know Jesus as their personal Lord and Savior.[3]

Obviously, it's easy to admire Billy Graham, and to be inspired by everything God did through him. For me, I always find myself inspired by one of his quotes:

"The greatest legacy one can pass on to one's children and grandchildren is not money or other

material things accumulated in one's life, but rather a legacy of character and faith."[4]

Billy Graham had more success than most pastors could ever think of having. God used him in extraordinary ways. I mean, 2.2 million people will experience Heaven as a result of his ministry! But even though he had success, it's not what he sought. In that quote, he gives us a lesson about priorities.

Money and material things are producers of popularity. While Billy Graham obtained some of these things, they aren't what motivated him. They didn't consume his focus. They were never the goal.

Character and faith are products of purpose. As you seek after God and everything that he has for you, they are naturally produced. These are the things that Billy valued, that drove him, and kept him moving forward.

He made sure that his priorities revolved around purposeful things rather than popular things. It's not that popularity is never attached to purpose because sometimes it is. But popularity is a dangerous goal, because even if it's achieved for a time, it will always fade. Living a life of purpose will require you to prioritize character and faith over material or temporal things, but they will last forever.

DO YOUR PRIORITIES REVOLVE AROUND POPULAR THINGS OR PURPOSEFUL THINGS?

Billy Graham chased purpose over popularity, and his life had eternal impact.

Bartimaeus ignored popularity as he continued to pursue Jesus, and it led him closer to his miracle.

Jesus, when he walked this planet, had moments of extreme popularity. But when he fulfilled his purpose and went to the cross, the crowds disappeared. Only a few of his faithful followers were there with him. Most, out of doubt or fear, abandoned him.

Your miracle, and your impact on humanity, is dependent upon choosing purpose over popularity once God shows up at the wayside of your life.

SEVEN

REFLECTION + APPLICATION

In general, are you more motivated by popularity or purpose?

_____

_____

_____

From the list in this chapter, do you have any of the qualities of a person who seeks popularity? Invite God into that area. What might he be asking you to change?

_____

_____

_____

Is God your number one priority? Ask him to help you set aside anything in your life that comes before him.

_____

_____

_____

What is your purpose? If you don't know, continue to dive into God's Word. Ask God to show you who he is calling you to become and what he wants you to accomplish.

_____

_____

_____

CHAPTER EIGHT

THROW OFF YOUR COAT

BARTIMAEUS THREW ASIDE HIS BEGGAR'S COAT, JUMPED UP, AND CAME TO JESUS.

MARK 10:50

To those of you who have stuck with me this long, congratulations! In my opinion, we are about to explore the most powerful moment in this story.

It's almost time for Bartimaeus to receive his miracle! As Jesus called him to come over, Bartimaeus did something interesting as he went. He threw aside his beggar's coat.

On the surface, it doesn't seem like that big of a deal. He took off his coat, so what? Maybe he was hot. Maybe it was unstylish and he didn't want to wear it during the most meaningful moment of his life. Maybe he was embarrassed about it and didn't want Jesus to see it.

The reality is that Bartimaeus' coat was the most important thing he owned.

Tons of people were pouring in to live in Roman territory at this time because of their advancements as a society. As we talked about earlier, one of their most impressive developments was their road system. However, the new roads in heavily populated cities would get crowded with beggars, as it was their best chance to make some serious cash.

To bring order and keep the roads from being overrun, the Romans created one of the first welfare systems. It worked like this: if you were unemployed for whatever reason or couldn't earn a living, then you would have to go to the government and apply for a beggar's coat. These coats were not issued to just anybody. They were only given to those deemed incapable of providing for themselves – usually the handicapped, disabled, or widowed.

A beggar's coat legitimized you as a beggar. It permitted you to beg for what you needed to survive. When Roman citizens saw the beggar's coat, they knew that person was allowed to receive donations. If a beggar didn't have the coat, they couldn't make any money and would probably die.

So the coat that Bartimaeus threw aside was not just any old coat. It wasn't to keep him warm. It wasn't a fashion statement (even though wearing layers always makes you look better). His identity and security were completely wrapped up within this coat. Without it, he couldn't eat. If it was lost, he wouldn't be able to survive!

Considering there were large crowds following Jesus, when Bartimaeus threw off his coat, it probably got trampled on and lost among the people. Most likely, he would never see it again.

That put Bartimaeus in a tough position. He obviously believed, hoped, and expected Jesus to restore his eyesight, but...what if he didn't? Bartimaeus would be left with no options!

Yet, when Jesus called him, Bartimaeus tossed the coat aside. He threw away the thing that he was completely dependent on.

Why?

I don't think Bartimaeus was being careless; he was making a statement. He wanted Jesus to know he no longer needed Plan B because he fully trusted whatever plans Jesus had for him. He became independent of everything the world had to offer him as he became fully dependent on Jesus. He wasn't just leaving his coat behind...

He was leaving his old identity behind.

He was leaving his old security behind.

He was leaving his old habits behind.

He was leaving his old means of survival behind.

He was leaving his old life behind.

He was leaving the wayside behind.

What Bartimaeus realized in the pursuit of his miracle is the same thing that we need to realize as we chase after ours:

IF WE EVER WANT TO THRIVE WITH GOD, WE MUST FIRST LET GO OF OUR MEANS TO SURVIVE ON OUR OWN.

For Bartimaeus, the beggar's coat represented the life he was comfortable living. Begging beside a ditch of human waste was his everyday reality. It was what he was used to waking up and doing every single day. To him, it had become second nature.

It's hard for some of us to imagine begging for a living to be comfortable because to us it sounds so dysfunctional. However, it's human nature to become comfortable with our dysfunctions. Living in insecurity is dysfunctional, but people still accept insecurity as their identity. Depression and anxiety are dysfunctional, yet people still learn to live with it. Sin is dysfunctional but it's still a source of security for so many people.

What is comfortable for us isn't always God's best for us. Often we have to leave what is comfortable to see God move in our lives. We must leave the old behind before we step into the new.

Colossians 3:9-10 says,

For you have stripped off your old sinful nature and all its wicked deeds. Put on your new nature, and be renewed as you learn to know your Creator and become like him.

When you become serious about following Jesus, he will invite you to put away old things for new ones. To put away old habits for new disciplines. To toss aside old fears for new adventures. To get rid of old sin and discover a new freedom. To put away the old you and be more like him.

WE MUST
LEAVE
BEHIND
THE OLD
BEFORE
WE STEP
INTO
THE NEW

Just like Bartimaeus took off his old coat, Colossians encourages us to take off our old selves. In the same way he walked toward Jesus and a chance for a new life, we are urged us to move toward Jesus and a new way of life!

Many of us want a miracle for our lives. Some of us *need* a miracle in our lives. However, miracles don't often happen on our terms.

MIRACLES DON'T HAPPEN WITHIN THE CONFINES OF COMFORT ZONES.

When you look at the ministry of Jesus, people often received miracles when they left their comfort zones. Whether it was Bartimaeus, the woman with the issue of blood,[1] the paralyzed man lowered through the roof,[2] or the ten lepers,[3] people experienced miracles when they left their comfort zones and walked toward Jesus.

Jesus will meet you in the middle of your mess. He stopped at the wayside for Bartimaeus, but then Jesus called him to come *out* of the wayside.

After you shout for mercy to get you out of your mess, when you cry out for more than what you're living now, Jesus will stand right outside the perimeter of your comfort zone and invite you to come. He invites you to step outside of what you've always known and become completely dependent on him in the unknown.

That's where Bartimaeus discovered his miracle. And that's where you will discover yours.

UNREASONABLE OBEDIENCE

I still remember the day I quit my job at the steel mill.

I started working there at eighteen years old. When you live in blue-collar, Youngstown, Ohio, some of the best jobs that you can get are in manufacturing. You don't have to have an education – which was perfect for me, because I didn't. The only qualification you needed is a willingness to work a lot of hours.

It was the first time that I ever had an "adult job." I went from flipping burgers at McDonald's, making minimum wage, to big paychecks and benefits at the mill.

For being only eighteen years old, this was a great gig. The job came with good benefits, incentive programs, and a retirement plan. Even though it wasn't my favorite work in the world, I figured that I was set for the rest of my life. It might seem silly, but I was making more money than I ever thought I'd be able to in life. I began to find my identity in the cash flow I had and the lifestyle I could live because of it.

I lived by the "if you like it, buy it" budget. If I saw shoes I liked, I bought them. If I saw clothes I liked, I bought them. I hated doing laundry so much (what eighteen-year-old guy likes to do laundry?) that I would just go to the store and buy new clothes instead of washing the ones I had. A lot of my friends were in college and only worked a couple of hours a week, or not at all. I became the guy who would pay for all of them and show them a good time – which of course made them my *really* good friends in that season! The point is, I didn't know how to manage my money and grew accustomed to living my version of a lavish lifestyle.

In that same season of my life, I was presented with an opportunity to go to bible college. I hadn't been following Jesus for that long, but I knew that God was inviting me to do this. I knew it was really a desire of my heart. However, to attend bible college, I'd have to give up my job at the mill. I'd have to sacrifice my income, benefits, and lifestyle.

Even though I wanted to go, at the same time, I didn't want to! I remember the tension of feeling the call of God, but not wanting to give up what had become so comfortable to me.

On the day I went into the mill to quit my job, I remember the uneasiness of walking away from security and into the unknown. I was consumed with "what ifs."

Anytime you follow Jesus into the unknown, you will always have to walk past "what ifs."

What if it doesn't work out?

What if I'm not pastor material?

What if I go broke and end up on the street?

What if I didn't hear God correctly?

What if my friends don't want to be my friends anymore?

What if I'm being an idiot?

If you stop at every "what if," you'll never experience everything that God has for your life. He never lays out every step of the plan for you before you say yes. If we knew exactly where we were going, we wouldn't need a Guide. God wants you to simply obey and follow, and build trust in him along the way. His mercy is on the other side of "what if."

So I moved past the "what ifs" and went to bible college. And I have to be honest with you, it was tough. I went from spending money on whatever I wanted, whenever I wanted, to only spending $5 per day on food. Most days, I had to share that money with my friend Mark, who had no money to spend on food. We found ourselves at McDonald's, where I used to work, almost every day. We would both get two Dollar Menu sandwiches and split a fountain drink. And that had to hold us over for the entire day!

But here's why I did it: I knew that where I was going was better than where I had been.

Looking back, even though it was challenging, I'm glad that I was willing to step out of my comfort zone. I'm thankful that God gave me the strength to move past the "what ifs." There are miracles in my life and the lives of others that would not have happened if I hadn't trusted his plan.

I wouldn't be married to Steph.

I wouldn't have been blessed with my children.

Rust City Church wouldn't exist.

I'd have never met some of my best friends.

There are lives that might not have been changed.

My old pastor, Rod Parsley, said it best:

"WHEN GOD GIVES A WORD, REASON IS NOT REQUIRED."

We naturally look to our reason to help us make decisions. We consider all of the "what ifs" because we think rationally. Our ability to reason makes us human; however, when God shows up and invites us to something new, it challenges our reasoning. Sometimes it doesn't make sense at all. The reality is that God is often unreasonable!

The Bible is full of God making unreasonable requests. He asked Abraham to leave the security of his home to go to "a land he would later show him" so that he could become "the father of many nations."[4] Abraham – who by the way had zero kids at the time – had to pack up his life and move without even knowing where he was headed. That's unreasonable!

God asked Noah to build an ark to prepare for the flooding of the entire earth even though rain was not common in that day. That seems like an unreasonable request.

God called Paul to be an apostle and plant churches, even though he was known for his cold-blooded persecution and assassination of Christians. That doesn't even make sense!

In spite of how things looked, Bartimaeus, Noah, Abraham, Paul, and so many others chose to follow the words that God had spoken to them rather than their ability to reason and rationalize. Because of their faith in God's words, miracles followed their obedience.

If you're reading this, maybe there's something specific that God has called you to be or to do. It's probably something that terrifies you. Maybe you haven't yet stepped into it because your reasoning has been telling you not to do it.

I want to encourage you, when God truly speaks to you, reason is not required. In Isaiah 55:8-9, the Lord says:

> *"My thoughts are nothing like your thoughts, and my ways are far beyond anything you could imagine. For just as the heavens are higher than the earth, so my ways are higher than your ways and my thoughts higher than your thoughts."*

What God is saying might not make sense to you right now, but he doesn't play by our rules – he's God! It's time for you to throw aside your coat of reason and run to where Jesus is leading you. It's time for you to say, "I don't know how this is going to work. I don't know how God is going to bring it all together. But, Lord, I will move according to the word that you spoke."

It will be uncomfortable. It will be scary. It will challenge you and stretch you beyond belief. But it will be worth it.

EARTHLY VS ETERNAL

Jim Elliot grew up as a young boy who longed to be a missionary. He would listen to the stories of the missionaries who visited his church and knew that's what he wanted to do when he got older. His heart burned with passion for people who lived in parts of the world that had never heard about Jesus.

At twenty-five years old, his dream became a reality as he left the comfort of America and sailed to Quito, Ecuador. There he learned how to speak Spanish before moving to Shandi, where there was a small village full of people who didn't know about the love of Jesus. In the few years Jim spent there, he watched as Jesus transformed the entire village and many of the locals became Christians.

In 1956, Jim felt God tugging on his heart once again. He knew that it was time to move and set up camp in the territory of the Aucas, a dangerous and uncivilized tribe in Ecuador. The Aucas had been known for showing violence and hostility, especially toward outsiders. Even though it didn't sound reasonable, Jim, his wife Elisabeth, and their team set up camp on a beach near where the Aucas lived.

The Aucas had recently killed several workers from an oil drilling company nearby. Everybody had moved away from them because they were afraid of being murdered. Jim knew that the only way to stop the violence was to bring them into an encounter with the love of Jesus. Trusting the word that God had spoken, they moved towards the people from whom everyone else was moving away.

Jim and his team brought gifts to the Aucas and started building trust with them. It seemed as if a genuine relationship was starting to develop. Some of the Aucas would come to the beach where Jim and his team lived and share meals with them. One day, Jim asked them to bring more of their friends next time.

A couple of days later, when two Auca women walked out of the jungle and showed up on the beach, Jim was excited. He grabbed his team, waved, and started walking over to the women, but quickly realized that the women weren't friendly. As Jim and his team turned to retreat, they found themselves surrounded by a group of Auca warriors with spears raised. Jim started to reach for his gun but decided against using it. He knew that showing any violence against them, even in self-defense, would not advance the mission of showing them the love of Jesus. Even if he had to die, other missionaries would be able to come and build upon what Jim and his team started.

Seconds later, the Auca warriors threw their spears. Jim and four of his team members were instantly killed. Jim's wife and a few other members of the team survived, as they weren't on the beach when the warriors attacked, but it seemed their mission had ended tragically.

Less than two years later, Elisabeth Elliot and her daughter Valerie moved back to the Aucas village and were able to establish a home with some of the women. Eventually, because of the sacrificial love the men had shown before, many Aucas came to know Jesus, and the entire culture of their tribe was changed.

Jim Elliot's life inspired many, but his death inspired even more. He was willing to step out of his comfort zone even though it killed him. Because of his willingness to take a risk, an entire tribe of people is changed today. Jim is spending eternity in Heaven. He might even be there with some of the Auca warriors that he never even had the chance to meet. His worst "what if" came true, yet he still made an impact on this world that echoes throughout eternity.

One of my favorites quotes from Jim Elliot is this:

"HE IS NO FOOL WHO GIVES UP WHAT HE CANNOT KEEP TO GAIN THAT WHICH HE CANNOT LOSE."[5]

Jim gave up his earthly life. He understood that it wasn't his in the first place. And in giving up his life, he gained what he couldn't lose. Not only is he experiencing eternity with Jesus, but others are as well.

I believe that if we are going to leave the comforts of this life and pursue Jesus with everything that we have, we first have to shift our perspective. We have to lay down our earthly perspective and obtain a heavenly one.

Matthew 6:19-20 says,

Don't store up treasures here on earth, where moths eat them and rust destroys them, and where thieves break in and steal. Store your treasures in heaven, where moths and rust cannot destroy, and thieves do not break in and steal.

The comfort that we desire on earth is temporary. The favorite sweatshirt, the freshly baked bread (we're not supposed to eat them, but I know we all still love carbs), the warm bed, the padded bank account, the Instagram followers – all of it will eventually cease to exist. However, when we step out of our comfort and follow Jesus, he develops eternal things on the inside of us. He establishes eternity in us while we live on the earth. Our life becomes not just about us, but about the eternal impact that we can have on those around us.

Renown author, C.S. Lewis, wrote:

> *If you read history you will find that the Christians who did most for the present world were precisely those who thought most of the next. It is since Christians have largely ceased to think of the other world that they have become so ineffective in this.*[6]

Are you more focused on what you can achieve here and now, or on how your here-and-now will live on? Holding on to the comforts of this life will keep you from the abundance of new life in Christ.

Jim Elliot stepped out of his comfort zone, knowing it might lead to the end of his life on earth, fully aware that it might be the last time he saw his wife and baby. Even though we see what he gave up, I think we can only see a small piece of what was gained.

What comfort zones might God be asking you to step out of? What might he be asking you to leave behind?

THROW YOUR COAT ASIDE

Bartimaeus threw off his beggar's coat. He didn't need it anymore. His desire for Jesus was greater than the desire for where he had been. The comfort of his coat couldn't compare to the call of God. And I can guarantee that the comfort God gives, even in the scariness of your calling, is so much more powerful than any false sense of comfort you can find on this planet.

What "coat" do you need to throw aside as you follow Jesus?

Maybe it's time for you to throw aside the coat of fear that you've been wearing.

Perhaps it's time to cast off the coat of depression that has consumed your life.

You've outgrown the coat of complacency that you've worn every day. It's time to finally get rid of it.

God is calling you away from comfort. He's calling you away from the dysfunction, sin, and perceived security. He might be calling you away from the job that you've always known or relationships that you've always had.

He's calling you to become completely independent from the things of this world in order to become completely dependent on him. Will you leave your coat behind and answer the call?

EIGHT

REFLECTION + APPLICATION

Have you become comfortable with things that are dysfunctional in your life? Ask God to reveal anything inside of you that doesn't look like him.

_____

_____

_____

_____

What are the "what ifs" that are limiting you right now? Instead of imagining the worst, ask God to help you envision the amazing things that could happen if you follow him!

_____

_____

_____

_____

Does your perspective tend to be earthly or eternal (selfish or selfless)? In what ways might you be able to have an eternal impact on the people around you?

_____

_____

_____

_____

CHAPTER NINE

WHAT DO YOU WANT?

"WHAT DO YOU WANT ME TO DO FOR YOU?" JESUS ASKED. "MY RABBI," THE BLIND MAN SAID. "I WANT TO SEE!"

MARK 10:51

Bartimaeus caught the attention of Jesus by shouting. Out of compassion, Jesus called him over. In faith, Bartimaeus left behind his coat and his old life.

But then Jesus asked this question: *What do you want me to do for you?*

Uh, hello? He's a blind beggar.

What do you think he wants?

Why would Jesus ask Bartimaeus this question? I think it's pretty obvious to everyone what Bartimaeus needed! His biggest issue, the one that affected everything about his life, was his blindness. Jesus was in the business of opening blind eyes – he had a perfect track record – and Bartimaeus needed to see.

Jesus already knew what was best for Bartimaeus. Trust me, if you and I know what Bartimaeus needed,

Jesus in all of his infinite wisdom knew, too.

In Matthew 6:8, when talking about making requests to God, Jesus said: "your Father knows exactly what you need even before you ask him!"

Jesus didn't have to ask, but he did.

I believe he asked what Bartimaeus wanted because he wanted to hear his response.

Bartimaeus could have asked for anything. He could have asked for an easy way out, or maybe a large amount of money so he wouldn't have to beg anymore. He could have asked for something reasonable, maybe for somebody to take him into their home and give him a place to sleep at night. He could have asked for emotional comfort, hoping that Jesus would tell the people of Jericho to start treating him better.

But Bartimaeus didn't ask for any of that. He asked to see. He asked for something that wasn't easy, practical, or reasonable. He asked for the impossible.

There's something that we can learn about the way Jesus works in this story. He has the power to give you a miracle at any moment, but he wants to see that you have the faith for one first. He can change the course of your life in a split second. Seriously, he can do more in an instant than you can with all of your effort throughout your entire lifetime. However, he wants to see if you are willing to ask for the impossible.

WHAT YOU ASK OF JESUS SAYS A LOT ABOUT HOW MUCH YOU BELIEVE IN HIM.

Jesus' goal for your life is to get you to a place where one hundred percent of your faith is in him. He wants you to fully understand who he is and what he has the power to do, so you will fully surrender everything to him. God doesn't just show up and "fix your problems." He wants to fix your heart. The closer our hearts grow to God's heart, the more what we want will line up with what he wants. Then we can ask him for anything in his name and he will do it.[1]

While he absolutely has the power to do the miraculous on the external – healing, deliverance, restoration – he also wants to increase the faith that we have on the internal. He wants to develop us to a point where we dare to ask the impossible.

Bartimaeus had faith for the impossible, and therefore the impossible was done.

MALL-SIZED FAITH

I'll never forget when we first wanted to move our church to a new space.

We launched in an upstairs conference room inside a small office building. The maximum capacity for the room was 50 people and we were squeezing in more than 80 in each service over the weekend. During worship, you could feel the room shaking as people sang out praise to God and bounced to the beat – and our team would pray that we wouldn't fall through the floor! Ready or not, we needed a new location.

We prayed and asked God to guide us in our search

for a building. Every day, people from our church were texting and emailing me different locations. However, as we looked at buildings all over the area, nothing seemed suitable. There was no peace, and we were starting to get antsy.

As I continued to press into God, there was only one location that felt right. Of course, it was the scariest one – I wouldn't expect anything less out of God! So, I went to the largest mall in our county and asked if they had any available spaces to rent.

With mall trends on the decline for most of the 21st century, spaces previously occupied by large stores were becoming available. Our local mall had such a space available for us to consider. On the outside, this storefront was perfectly located. It was a corner space across the parking lot from the most popular retailer in our area, not to mention, the stadium of our city's minor league baseball team. Every day and every night, thousands of shoppers and baseball fans would see our church as they traveled to and from their activities.

It was a highly trafficked area in a landmark location for our community. I felt God speaking to me that if we put a church in a location where it didn't belong, he would reach people who felt like they didn't belong in church. That's a word that we still stand on today.

We were excited, at least until we saw the inside. It was much larger than we had envisioned. Every single square foot was a mess. Not only was I concerned about being able to fill it up, but I also was concerned about how much it would cost to renovate such a large space.

Everywhere I looked, all I could see were dollar bills. It would cost hundreds of thousands of dollars in necessary improvements.

At this time, our church had a little over 100 people attending, and most of them were young adults. If you know anything about young adults, they bring a lot of energy but not much cash! There was no way that our church had pockets deep enough to pull off moving into this space.

At the same time, another church in the community offered us the use of their space for free. It was in a small, rural area. It was a great church, but also very traditional. It felt like a church more for people who "belonged" in church, if you know what I mean. Plus, the space was large enough for our current size but didn't leave much room for growth. Still, it was free. In the church world, free is always good!

As I weighed various factors and prayed to God about both options, I continuously felt God stirring my heart about the mall space. A lot of my team did not sense that same stirring! The size scared them. The required renovations freaked them out. And the money needed seemed insurmountable. Many of them felt it'd be a safer next step to use the other church's space for free. With my rational brain, I agreed with them. But in my spirit, I had peace about acquiring the mall space.

In all the confusion, I remember talking to God, "On paper, this doesn't make sense, but it feels right. Will you show up and do the impossible?"

Looking back years later, I can tell you, not only did

God show up and meet our expectations, he blew them away. Volunteers came to help renovate the space, saving us thousands of dollars in labor expenses. Money came in from unexpected places. God provided in a way that we couldn't have done for ourselves.

I remember setting up chairs in the auditorium the day before the opening of our new building. I remember looking around a room that was more than double the size needed for our attendance at that time. In a moment of panic, I thought there was no way we'd fill it up – not just at our launch – *ever*!

Opening weekend, there was standing room only at our two services. Since then, we've had between three and five services every weekend at that campus. We've launched three more campuses, and we had to renovate the mall space again to make our auditorium even bigger. People who feel like they don't belong in church continue to come to our church!

I'm so glad I had the faith to believe God for the impossible. If I wouldn't have trusted where he was leading us, we might not have received what God wanted to give us all along.

On the wall of our staff offices, we have a huge print of one of my favorite scriptures. It has become the driving force behind our church, team, and every decision that we make:

WHAT IS IMPOSSIBLE WITH MAN IS POSSIBLE WITH GOD.[2]

Things that you can't do, God can! He can move mountains that you can't budge. He can heal sickness from which you can't recover. He can operate through you in a way that is so much greater than the talent you have.

What's impossible for you is possible for him. He's waiting on you to ask.

PRAYING IMPOSSIBLE PRAYERS

Let's get practical. As we said earlier, what you ask God for says a lot about the amount of faith that you have in him. Do you believe that God is who he says he is? Do you believe he will do what he says he'll do?

This is one reason why it's so important to study the Bible and get God's words in your heart. If you don't have that foundation of truth to stand on, it will be hard to pray and see God move, because you won't be confident in his character, his desires, his promises, or his track record.

Jesus tells his disciples (and us) in John 16:23 (TPT),

"Until now you've not been bold enough to ask the Father for a single thing in my name, but now you can ask, and keep on asking him! And you can be sure that you'll receive what you ask for, and your joy will have no limits!"

If you want to evaluate how big your faith in God is, look at the type of prayers that you pray. Your prayers will reveal the condition of your heart. If you have a genuine relationship with Jesus, you should pray without doubting his name (i.e., who he is and what he can do).

Our prayers, if our belief is correctly placed, shouldn't be practical or rational. They should be bold, but they need to be even more than that. They need to be impossible.

Let's look at some qualities of impossible prayers.

1. IF GOD DOESN'T SHOW UP, IT WON'T WORK.

In John 15:5, Jesus explains the importance of staying relationally connected to him. He says,

> *"Yes, I am the vine; you are the branches. Those who remain in me, and I in them, will produce much fruit. For apart from me you can do nothing."*

Jesus compares himself to a vine and us to the branches. Think of a grape vine. If a branch stays connected to the vine, you'll see grapes growing on it, but if it doesn't stay attached, if it gets broken or cut off, it won't grow anything. All of the nutrients and hydration that a branch needs to produce fruit come from the vine. In other words, Jesus is our source! If we don't stay connected to him, we won't see the fruit of him working through our lives.

The last part of that verse always struck me. Jesus says that without him, we can do nothing. It's not that we can literally do nothing, but anything that is of eternal value can't be produced on our own.

Jesus wants to do miraculous things in and through our lives. But, in no way, shape, or form, can we see the miraculous apart from him. It only happens when we remain connected.

God has put us in a position where we have to be completely dependent on him. That means when we pray, we should do so with complete dependency on him. If he doesn't show up, it doesn't work. But if he is in the center of it, he will make everything work together for good and for his glory![3]

A couple verses later, in John 15:7 (TPT), Jesus says,

"But if you live in life-union with me and if my words live powerfully within you—then you can ask whatever you desire and it will be done."

Live with your life so intertwined with Jesus that you can't even tell where he begins and you end. Learn to speak his words and make them a part of you. Nothing in your life or your prayers will "work" if you don't stay connected to God as your source. But if you do, you're on your way to seeing impossible prayers answered!

2. WHAT I'M ASKING FOR IS NOT WITHIN THE SCOPE OF MY NATURAL ABILITY.

God has blessed all of us with some really cool gifts and abilities. You have talents and skills that are unique to you. You use the way that you were created to function in society, communicate with people, and provide for yourself. However, your natural gifts cannot produce supernatural results.

When you pray bold prayers, you cannot naturally do what you are asking for on your own. You will need the help of the Holy Spirit as you move toward a miracle. You won't be able to accomplish it with your own strength or ability.

When we receive the Holy Spirit, we gain access to *his* supernatural power, wisdom, and strength. He also gives us at least one spiritual gift, to equip us to help others and bring glory to God.[4]

For example, if you have a life-altering decision to make, you will need God's Spirit to download wisdom on the inside of you. If you are believing for the healing of a friend, you will need his healing power to work through you. As you are chasing your God-given destiny, you will need faith that can only come from him!

Impossible prayers are answered supernaturally. Therefore, we have to pray beyond the scope of our natural ability.

3. WHAT I'M ASKING FOR TAKES IMAGINATION TO ENVISION.

By nature, our Creator is a bigger thinker than we are. He thought up the entire universe and everything in it in seven days. Most of the time I can't even remember what I did seven days ago! God exists outside of time, so he sees everything – past, present, future – all at once.

It's no surprise that we think smaller than God does. But that means, if we aren't careful, what we ask him for will be limited to the confines of our own minds. If we are going to pray impossible prayers, we have to access the mind of Christ. 1 Corinthians 2:16 says:

Who can know the LORD's thoughts? Who knows enough to teach him? But we understand these things, for we have the mind of Christ.

When we talk with God, we should ask him to help us think and see like he does. Rather than settling for what we can naturally envision, we should dig into his imagination and his word to think bigger! Ephesians 3:20 (TPT) says it like this:

Never doubt God's mighty power to work in you and accomplish all this. He will achieve infinitely more than your greatest request, your most unbelievable dream, and exceed your wildest imagination!

4. I'M AFRAID OF WHAT I'M ASKING.

I mentioned earlier that when we chose to move our church into the local mall, I had enough faith to pray for the impossible. While that's the truth, I don't want you to get the wrong idea. I still felt nervous as could be. I continually had to stop myself from worrying about everything that could go wrong. I was terrified of the very thing that I asked.

Faith is not believing God for the impossible in the absence of fear, it's trusting God even in the face of fear! Faith is standing on who God is and what his word says even when you aren't sure about your present reality.

Most of the time, fear comes when we're focusing on our own ability instead of God's. When we've prayed for something crazy, and God starts to unfold the plans, we start to doubt ourselves because we realize – I CAN'T DO THIS! But that's just the point. You can't. God can. You have to rely on God every single step of the way, not just in the beginning, but until the very end.

Fear is not an indication that we shouldn't ask for something, but that we should ask for the very thing of which we are afraid. It's not a warning sign to turn around; it's confirmation that you are headed in the right direction. Trust that God will continue to do the impossible. What he starts, he is faithful to finish.

ACTIVATING HIS POWER

When Jesus asked Bartimaeus what he wanted, the blind man asked for the impossible: I want to see.

The reality is, if Jesus didn't respond to his request, Bartimaeus would have stayed blind. This was beyond the scope of what he could accomplish on his own.

Maybe when Bartimaeus woke up that day, he was so accustomed to his misery that the thought of being able to see wasn't even in his mind. But when he heard that Jesus was near, his imagination was stirred for bigger and better things.

Even though he didn't know what life would look like afterward, he asked God anyway. Fear was undoubtedly present on the inside of him – if his prayer was answered, what then? Would he be able to earn a living? Was he even good at anything? But none of this stopped Bartimaeus from praying an impossible prayer.

What kind of prayers are you praying?

Are they safe?

Are they practical?

Are they reasonable?

Or are you really believing for the impossible?

Some of you have given up on your marriage because too much has gone wrong, and you aren't sure if the effort you put forth will be reciprocated. You have access to ask God for what seems impossible!

Some of you need healing in your body. Maybe you haven't been praying for it because you're afraid of disappointment, or even afraid of what life will be like without your ailment. Don't be afraid to ask God for the impossible and trust that out of the love he has for you, he will take care of you.

Some of you reading this have unfulfilled dreams. Maybe you haven't believed for God to do the impossible because you don't know if you have what it takes to accomplish what he's calling you to do. Here's my encouragement: you *don't* have what it takes. (Sorry, was that not encouraging? wait for it...) What's impossible for you is *possible with God*. His power can show up and work in and through you!

John 3:30, one of my favorite verses, says,

HE MUST BECOME GREATER AND GREATER, AND I MUST BECOME LESS AND LESS.

God wants to invite you to stop focusing on your strength and start focusing on his. Where your power stops is where God's power starts. As long as you only ask for what seems obtainable, you will only experience what you can do. But when you have faith for the impossible, you'll see what God can do, and miracles will unfold in your life.

NINE
REFLECTION+APPLICATION

What is a miracle that God has done in your life? Think about it and reflect on the impossible things he can do.

_____

_____

_____

_____

Do you ask God for impossible things? What are some things that prevent you from doing so?

_____

_____

_____

_____

Ask God to give you a vision for something that seems impossible to you!

_____

_____

_____

_____

CHAPTER TEN

MERCY > MESS

AND JESUS SAID TO HIM, "GO, FOR YOUR FAITH HAS HEALED YOU." INSTANTLY THE MAN COULD SEE, AND HE FOLLOWED JESUS DOWN THE ROAD.

MARK 10:52

Before we go any further, give yourself a round of applause. You've stayed with me, and Bartimaeus, over the course of this entire journey. That is something to celebrate. And as long as we are cheering for ourselves, we have to cheer for Bartimaeus as well. He finally got his miracle! His sight was finally restored.

I love that it took us until the last chapter of this book to get to the miracle. I think that sometimes when we read the Bible, the only thing we remember are the miracles themselves, but every miracle has a journey attached to it. Typically, it's a journey of faith.

Let's recap for a moment.

On this particular day, Bartimaeus was not intentionally seeking a miracle. He woke up just as he had every other morning, not realizing that his life would change forever. He took his spot by the wayside. It was a location where he was used to spending his time. He didn't even notice the smell anymore. He was completely unaware of the symbolism. He had no clue that thousands of years later, the place where he sat would become the title of somebody's book. He went to the wayside because that was his routine. Sit, beg, repeat.

However, in the middle of the mundane, he heard a buzz throughout the crowd. As he asked around, he found out the miracle worker from Nazareth was passing through the city! In an instant, Bartimaeus decided that he couldn't let him pass without at least trying to get his attention. He started shouting.

As he called out to Jesus, people tried to shush him. People typically weren't very supportive of him. He wasn't surprised or deterred.

As he shouted again, he gave it everything he had. With boldness in his voice, he begged for mercy. He was used to begging, but this time it was different. This wasn't just about money or food. From all he'd heard about Jesus – this was the Messiah!

There was urgency in his shout; this chance wouldn't come again. Bartimaeus didn't know if he could even be heard above the noise of the crowd swarming Jesus. Even if Jesus heard the shouting, he might not be able to tell where it was coming from. And after all, he was a busy man, constantly traveling from city to city, probably preoccupied with ministry and tired from performing so many miracles.

But to everyone's surprise, Jesus stopped! He stopped and he called Bartimaeus to come to him. It's funny how quickly everyone around Bartimaeus changed their tune. Now they were excited for him. Yet Bartimaeus didn't have time to waste evaluating whether his actions were or were not pleasing to the people; he had a meeting with Jesus.

He threw his beggar's coat aside. That coat had meant a lot to him. It's how he made money. It was his only hope to get a good meal. Heck, it was the way he survived. But in his excitement, he tossed it aside, making a declaration that he didn't need it anymore. He didn't want survival; he wanted the Savior.

When Jesus asked Bartimaeus what he wanted, he dared to ask for the impossible. He didn't want food stamps or a place to stay, he wanted to see. And it all finally paid off!

A JOURNEY OF FAITH

Mark writes that Jesus healed Bartimaeus instantly because it all happened so fast. In one moment, Bartimaeus couldn't see, and the next moment, he could. However, before Bartimaeus was instantly healed, he went on a journey of faith.

He had the faith to shout.

He had the faith to shout louder.

He had the faith to believe Jesus was the Son of God.

He had the faith to throw aside his beggar's coat.

He had the faith to ask for the impossible.

Every miracle is preceded by a journey of faith. Before Jesus restored Bartimaeus' sight, he let Bartimaeus and everybody else know that it was his faith that healed him. It's intriguing that Jesus didn't say, "I healed you." Even though we know that Jesus is the one who heals, he made sure to clarify that Bartimaeus' faith was a crucial element to his miracle.

Hebrews 11, the faith chapter of the Bible, defines faith as "the evidence of things we cannot see."

Martin Luther King, Jr. is attributed with saying, "Faith is taking the first step even when you don't see the whole staircase."[1]

Faith is chasing after something that you can't yet see. Faith is giving everything you have, even when you aren't sure how it's going to turn out.

Bartimaeus wasn't sure how things were going to turn out. He knew what he wanted to happen, but had no way of knowing if that's what would actually happen. What if he asked for a miracle and walked away still not being able to see? With everyone watching, the crowds would have begun to ridicule him again or pushed him back to the wayside.

But because he believed that Jesus was who he said he was, he continued to take steps of faith anyway. He continued to draw closer to Jesus in the midst of uncertainty.

MIRACLES DON'T JUST REQUIRE FAITH, THEY DEVELOP FAITH.

God will use your need for a miracle to draw you closer to himself. He does miracles in your life because of his love for you, but doing outward miracles is not his only goal. God's desire is for you to grow in loving him and walking with him down the road.

The journey to your miracle is a journey closer to Jesus, as he wants to live in intimate relationship with you. Hebrews 11:7 (TPT) says,

> For we come to God in faith knowing that he is real and that he rewards the faith of those who give all their passion and strength into seeking him.

God is not a magician. He doesn't just show up, do something impressive, and then move on. He is a miracle worker. He changes your circumstances because he wants to change your heart. He does miracles so that the two of you can build a closer relationship, as your faith in him increases.

FOLLOW

When Bartimaeus received his miracle, Jesus told him to go because his faith had healed him. However, Bartimaeus didn't go; he stayed with Jesus. He proceeded to follow him down the road.

Earlier, we talked about how Jesus responds to our hunger. I need to let you know that in the same way Jesus responds to us, we have a responsibility to respond to him!

WE LOVE WHEN JESUS RESPONDS TO US, AND JESUS LOVES WHEN WE RESPOND TO HIM.

How selfish would it have been if Bartimaeus received his sight and never acknowledged Jesus again? The entire narrative on Bartimaeus would have changed if he would have pursued God only when he needed something, then abandoned him once he got it.

The appropriate response to Jesus showing you mercy or doing the miraculous in your life is to *follow* him.

If I can be transparent, I see too many people who accept Jesus but never do life with him afterward. They pursue the miracle of eternal life, but neglect to make Jesus a part of their life on earth. They accept the fact that he died for them but they never live for him. Jesus is not interested in just being a "get out of hell" card.

Often, people will pray for healing, freedom from anxiety, or for a higher paying job. Those are great things to pray; God cares about every aspect of your life and wants to give you good things! But sometimes those same people never deal with the sin in their lives or the selfishness in their hearts. They don't view the mistakes they've made as mistakes. They choose to continue to sin even when the Holy Spirit convicts them. Jesus is not interested in simply winking at sin and letting you do as you please.

Don't misunderstand me; I don't believe that God is mad at you. I actually believe that he's mad about you. I believe that he is so crazy about you that he constantly wants what is best for you. He also knows that what is best for you can only be found on the journey of following him.

Trust me, I'm far from perfect. I mess up, make mistakes, and deal with sin in my life. I don't have it all figured out, but I have determined that, no matter what, I will continue to follow Jesus.

It takes a while to figure out how to live this new life. Chances are, you didn't get into those addictions or negative thought patterns or bad habits overnight, which means you might not get out of them overnight. Jesus helps to deliver and develop you as you follow. You might have issues now, but you don't have to have them forever!

In John 3, Jesus explains what it means to be "born again." When we accept a relationship with him, we are reborn, not physically, but spiritually. We receive the Holy Spirit, who is God living on the inside of us, guiding and helping us through life.[2] Being born again is an instantaneous miracle, and it's also a process.

Think about when a child is born. They have to learn how to crawl, then walk, then talk, then read and write – pretty much everything! In the same way, when you are spiritually reborn, the Holy Spirit wants to help you relearn how to do life. He will teach and empower you to live in freedom from sin, to love others, and chase after his purpose. This is what *following* looks like.

Jesus can open up blind eyes in an instant, as he did

with Bartimaeus, but often miracles happen as we follow.

Overcoming sin patterns we've lived with for years is a miracle!

Becoming a less angry person as we spend more time with God is a miracle!

Serving others and pointing them toward Jesus is a miracle!

Miracles unfold as you follow. If you don't follow Jesus down the road, you'll never know what else he has for you.

———

The biggest miracle in my life has been the opportunity to raise my children.

However, the first time I found out that Steph was pregnant, I was terrified! Most of my fear was because my biological father didn't raise me. He wasn't there for me because his dad wasn't there for him.

Even though I came from generations of fatherless men, my boys will never experience that. That generational curse ended with me. My kids will never know what it's like to not have a dad. And that is nothing short of a miracle.

Psalm 68:5 says God is "a father to the fatherless." I'm able to raise my kids because God stepped in where my father bowed out. God was an example not just of a good father, but the best father! However, I only experienced his fatherhood as I went on the journey of following him.

MIRACLES UNFOLD AS YOU FOLLOW

For as long as I've followed God, he has shown me what a loving Father is like. He helped me find my identity in his love. The entire time he was fathering me before my kids even existed, he was preparing me. He knew that someday I'd be able to extend the same love to my children that he had extended to me.

He was doing a miracle in my life without me even realizing it. It was a miracle that unfolded through following.

For those of you who are closely following Jesus right now, I hope that this gives you the perspective to realize that miracles are unfolding in your life without you even realizing it. And for those of you who aren't following him the way you could be, I hope that this gives you the courage to follow God more closely. The miracles that he has for your life are dependent on it!

DOWN THE ROAD

So where exactly did Bartimaeus follow Jesus?

Let's not forget that Jesus was on his way to Jerusalem, which means that he was walking to the place where he would die. Even though crowds of people surrounded Jesus now, soon most of them would disperse. And just as Jesus died an unfair death, there was a chance that anyone who remained by his side would die an unfair death as well.

Bartimaeus didn't just follow Jesus. He followed Jesus down the road to his death. Quite possibly, he follows Jesus to his own death.

The Bible contains some unique encouragement that Jesus gave his followers:

"Whoever wants to be my disciple must deny themselves and take up their cross daily and follow me." [3]

Most of us probably know that Jesus died on a cross. In those days, the cross was the most common and most painful way that Romans would execute criminals. It was a brutal public spectacle intended as a scare tactic to keep others from committing the same crimes and avoid paying the same price. Criminals would have to carry the huge, heavy cross beam down a crowded street, and then up a hill where their hands and feet would be nailed to the cross. They'd be lifted up for everyone to watch as they slowly died.

Jesus told his disciples that in order to follow him they'd have to take up their own cross – daily. This does not sound like the walk in the park some of us expect when we first give our lives to Jesus. He's supposed to fix everything and bring us out of the mess we're in and give us love and joy and peace! What is this about dying?!

This wasn't exactly what the first disciples were looking for either. They thought Jesus was going to deliver them from Roman oppression and establish himself as king, and that they'd get to sit on either side of his throne and be promoted to rule with him, gaining influence, status, and wealth. Instead, Jesus invited them to their deaths.

For them, physical death was actually a real possibility. Most of the original disciples were eventually martyred for their belief in Jesus. Most of us reading this are lucky enough to not have to worry about being killed for following Jesus. However, that doesn't mean that we are exempt from Jesus' command.

The invitation to follow Jesus is an invitation to die – not just to the power of sin,[4] but also to our selfish desires, our old ways. It's not until we die to ourselves that we can experience true life, abundant life, like Jesus promised.[5]

This might seem hard until we realize that, without Christ, we are already dead because of our sins. Without Jesus, we will continue to sit in our mess, wallow in our wayside, get comfortable in our crap, and never realize we were created for more. Ephesians 2:1-5 (TPT) says,

> *Even though you were once like corpses, dead in your sins and offenses...God still loved us with such great love. He is so rich in compassion and mercy. Even when we were dead and doomed in our many sins, he united us into the very life of Christ and saved us by his wonderful grace!*

So your options are death because of sin, or death *to* sin. In his mercy, Jesus offers new life, through dying to sin and self. What do you need to put to death today?

Some of you may need to die to negative thoughts. Others may need to die to secret sin. It's possible that you need to die self-doubt. Maybe you need to die to selfishness and start serving others (the local church is a great place to start!).

Whatever it is that you need to put to death, it's not until you're willing to die that you can fully live. True life is only found in following Jesus.

Right after Jesus gets to Jerusalem, knowing his time has come, he says:

> *"I tell you the truth, unless a kernel of wheat is planted in the soil and dies, it remains alone. But its death will produce many new kernels—a plentiful harvest of new lives. Those who love their life in this world will lose it. Those who care nothing for their life in this world will keep it for eternity. Anyone who wants to serve me must follow me..."* [6]

Following Jesus might not be the easy street we hoped, but there is so much more to be gained in eternity than what may be lost on earth.

———

Bartimaeus started the day by sitting in the wayside. He smelled the stank. He was surrounded by crap. He was right in the middle of a mess. It was the last place that he expected to find Jesus, yet Jesus showed up.

GOD'S MERCY WAS GREATER THAN HIS MESS.

And when Bartimaeus got his miracle, he followed Jesus down the road, never returning to the wayside again.

As I said before, this book is God showing up at the wayside of your life. You have it in your hands because God loves you, cares about you, and wants to do miracles in your life. In fact, I believe he's doing the miraculous right now in your heart as you read.

The question you have to answer is: will you return to the wayside? Will you go back to the old you, your old way of thinking, the bad habits, and unbelief? Or will you follow Jesus down the road, walk in his mercy and believe for the miraculous as you go?

If you don't have a relationship with Jesus, you can start one today! He came to this world, died for your sins, and rose from the grave so that you could have that relationship. He did for you what you couldn't do for yourself. Not only can you have eternal life with him because you are forgiven, but you can also do life with him daily as you "follow him down the road."

IF YOU WANT A FRESH START WITH JESUS, PRAY THIS PRAYER:
"Jesus, I know that you came to this world out of your love for me. You died on the cross and rose from the grave so that we could have a relationship. I believe you are God, and I believe that I can have a relationship with you. Today, I accept a fresh start. I no longer live for me, I live for you."

REFLECTION+APPLICATION

What steps of faith is God asking you to take as you move toward the miraculous things that he has for you?

_____

_____

_____

What miracles might God be doing that you haven't even recognized? Thank him that he is always working in your life.

_____

_____

_____

Are you following Jesus with everything that you have? What areas might you still need to surrender to him?

_____

_____

_____

Now that you've read this book, are you willing to call out to God at the wayside of your life?

_____

_____

_____

PROLOGUE
1. John 10:10 ESV

CHAPTER 1
1. 1 Samuel 16:7
2. Psalm 37:4 NIV
3. https://www.reference.com/world-view/many-verses-bible-a6bde39f20e77427

CHAPTER 2
1. Mark 10:46 DARBY, GNV, RGT use the word wayside
2. https://www.merriam-webster.com/dictionary/miracle
3. Exodus 14:31
4. This is a variation of something she heard Bill Johnson say
5. Hebrews 12:5-6 TPT

CHAPTER 3
1. 2 Samuel 7:12-13, Isaiah 9:7
2. Acts 7:49
3. Isaiah 53:5
4. Romans 8:34
5. Hebrews 4:15-16
6. https://www.dictionary.com/browse/pride
7. https://www.dictionary.com/browse/humility
8. Love Song for a Savior. Lyrics by Charlie Lowell, Dan Haseltine, Matt Bronleewe, Stephen Mason. ©1995 Bridge Building Music, Inc., Pogostick Music (Admin. by Brentwood-Benson Music Publishing, Inc.)
9. Lamentations 3:22-23

CHAPTER 4
1. Matthew 23:25-26
2. 1 Corinthians 13
3. Acts 1:8-9
4. https://en.wikipedia.org/wiki/Floyd_Mayweather_Jr._vs._Manny_Pacquiao
5. 1 Timothy 6:12
6. 1 Timothy 3:8-13
7. Matthew 12:24, Luke 11:14

CHAPTER 5

1. https://www.biography.com/athlete/mike-tyson
2. https://www.sun-sentinel.com/sports/fl-xpm-2012-11-09-sfl-mike-tyson-explains-one-of-his-most-famous-quotes-20121109-story.html
3. John 10:10
4. Matthew 7:11
5. Proverbs 29:18 KJV
6. Matthew 22:37-40
7. 1 Corinthians 12:4-11, Isaiah 43:7

CHAPTER 6

1. Ephesians 3:18-19
2. Mark 10:32-34
3. Matthew 20:34 TPT

CHAPTER 7

1. Matthew 6:24
2. https://billygraham.org/about/biographies/billy-graham
3. https://factsandtrends.net/2018/02/21/billy-grahams-life-ministry-by-the-numbers
4. https://billygraham.org/press-release/billy-graham-celebrates-93rd-birthday-following-release-of-30th-book-nearing-home/

CHAPTER 8

1. Mark 5:24-34
2. Mark 2:1-12
3. Luke 17:11-19
4. Genesis 12:1, 17:4
5. Jim Elliot, *The Journals of Jim Elliot* (Fleming H. Revell, 1978), p. 174
6. C.S. Lewis, *Mere Christianity* (San Francisco: HarperSanFrancisco, Harper edition, 2001), pp. 134-135.

CHAPTER 9

1. John 14:14
2. Luke 18:27 NIV
3. Romans 8:28
4. 1 Corinthians 12:7-11

CHAPTER 10

1. https://quoteinvestigator.com/2019/04/18/staircase/
2. John 14:16-17
3. Luke 9:23 NIV
4. Romans 6:7
5. John 10:10
6. John 12:24

GOD'S MERCY IS GREATER THAN MY MESS

DOUGGARASIC.COM